LAST DISCIPLE

LAST DISCIPLE

Lou Steel

XULON PRESS

Xulon Press
2301 Lucien Way #415
Maitland, FL 32751
407.339.4217
www.xulonpress.com

© 2022 by Lou Steel

All rights reserved solely by the author. The author guarantees all contents are original and do not infringe upon the legal rights of any other person or work. No part of this book may be reproduced in any form without the permission of the author.

Due to the changing nature of the Internet, if there are any web addresses, links, or URLs included in this manuscript, these may have been altered and may no longer be accessible. The views and opinions shared in this book belong solely to the author and do not necessarily reflect those of the publisher. The publisher therefore disclaims responsibility for the views or opinions expressed within the work.

Unless otherwise indicated, Scripture quotations taken from the New American Standard Bible (NASB). Copyright © 1960, 1962, 1963, 1968, 1971, 1972, 1973, 1975, 1977, 1995 by The Lockman Foundation. Used by permission. All rights reserved.

Scripture quotations taken from the King James Version (KJV)–*public domain.*

Scripture quotations taken from the New King James Version (NKJV). Copyright © 1982 by Thomas Nelson, Inc. Used by permission. All rights reserved.

Scripture quotations taken from the Holy Bible, New International Version (NIV). Copyright © 1973, 1978, 1984, 2011 by Biblica, Inc.™. Used by permission. All rights reserved.

Paperback ISBN-13: 978-1-66285-942-7
Hardcover ISBN- 13: 978-1-66288-590-7
Ebook ISBN-13: 978-1-66285-943-4

Dedication

This book is dedicated to those seeking an answer to the purpose of their life, where to find it, and how to defend against the slings and arrows of the enemy of our souls. You are not alone! The answer lies with our merciful and forgiving Lord and Savior. Jesus forgave us and we must forgive others, as well as ourselves. This is a crucial step in our spiritual growth often overlooked. Also, do not beat yourself up or dwell on your past sins. "It is finished!"

This book is also dedicated to all those whose paths we cross who are searching for peace beyond understanding and a way out of their struggles, addictions, and misery. We stand (and ride) with you! There is a way and a hope!

Lastly, this book is dedicated to those who are seeking a ministry through which to serve others rather than serving themselves but don't think they can. Be encouraged because you *can* do it!

Contents

Introduction ix
1. The Early Years BC 1
2. Rome 7
3. Back to the Homeland 11
4. Fast Forward 15
5. Speaking of God 25
6. Harley Davidson 29
7. Off to Sturgis 35
8. How About a Coffee? 38
9. Sharing the Faith 40
10. Finding our Place on the Battlefield 43
11. Hardcore 46
12. Enter the Last Disciples MC 50
13. Divine Intervention 55
14. Red & White, Ventura 63
15. Good to Go 71
16. Learning the Ropes 77
17. The Red & Gold – Red River Part I 80
18. Red River Part II 88
19. Triple Homicide at Rio Rancho 94
20. The Black & White 99
21. Laughlin River Rallies 104
22. Las Vegas Tension 106
23. The Blue & White 110
24. Reno Shootout 112

25. San Jose Shootout 114
26. The Phoenix 81 Connection. 117
27. Messaging the Spirit 139
28. Black & Gold Memorial 142
29. Street Vibes – Reno, NV 145
30. Cancer Scourge 150
31. "O Death where is Thy Sting?". 154
32. An Extra Rep for Jesus 164
33. Where Chapo Found God 167
34. Here we go again! 170
35. Fair Game 176
36. Wilfredo. 178
37. Terri's Fundraiser 181
38. Starbucks Meeting. 185
39. 5150 Todd. 188
40. Sweet Louise. 193
41. Listen to the Spirit but Look Out for the Devil!. 196
42. Hollister Runs and Shootouts at the Gas Pump. 200
43. The Greens – Crazy Dan 204
44. Greens in SoCal. 207
45. Last Disciples – East Side 209
46. Valley of the Shadow of Death 214
47. Hard to the Core 216
48. Reflections. 222
Acknowledgments 225

Introduction

This book is the true story of a man, his faith, and his spiritual journey, which led him (of all places) into the world of the outlaw biker. In this book, I will take you into that world and tell some of the amazing things I've witnessed, the "divine appointments" I've experienced, and the dangers and hardships I've encountered along the way.

I will also give a little background about myself to demonstrate the unlikelihood of where I ended up. As you read, it will become abundantly clear how God has intervened in my life and taken me in a direction that seemed not only eminently dangerous but so unlikely for a person of my background to accomplish "under my own power." This is how I came to realize the biblical truth that "... with God all things are possible" (Matthew 19:26, NIV).

I have changed some of the names in this book to provide privacy and safety to some of the people involved. Because it is sometimes considered disrespectful to use the names of the big, dominant motorcycle clubs, I instead refer to them by their club colors. Other than that, I have written the facts based on my journals, my best recollections, and my ability.

My purpose is to give testimony and hope to those who don't know God on a personal level, those who are agnostics, and those who simply and firmly don't believe there even *is* a God. It is written as much for them as it is for believers in God and followers of Jesus Christ. I will relate my experiences over the last twenty years and let the reader decide how it applies to them and their faith, or the lack thereof. I hope every reader will walk away with a stronger faith, a new attitude, and a new and joyful belief that God is real, He loves every one of you, and has a purpose for your life.

1
The Early Years BC

I was born in Bell, California on September 11, 1945. World War II had just ended. My father had originally been in the Army and then joined the Air Force when it first began. He went to Officer Candidate School (OCS) and became a flashy "Flyboy." He learned to fly in open-cockpit biplanes and wore a brown leather flight jacket, a padded leather flight helmet, and a white silk scarf. I remember when his flight logbook surpassed the one-year mark for piloting hours years later. He was raised as a German Lutheran farm boy in the little town of Hamler, Ohio.

Everyone on my mom's side of the family was Croatian and born into Catholicism. She grew up in Kansas City, Kansas, and was orphaned by age ten. Her aunt and uncle took her in and raised her. She was subsequently abused and beaten black and blue by her aunt and was kept home from school at times for fear of the nuns seeing her injuries. Decades later her aunt, who she called "Mom," asked her for forgiveness, which was given. Her Uncle Mike was a Kansas City police officer who eventually retired after forty-five years of service. He called my mom "Punkin" and thankfully never raised a hand to her.

Mom left home in Kansas by age seventeen and went to California to visit a cousin she considered a brother. It was in Los Angeles at the train station where she met my dad who was a "buck private" in the Army at the time. He was in battledress uniform and with a group of troops getting ready to deploy to Europe. World War ll ended at that very moment in time, so he never had to go. He and Mom went their separate ways as Mom returned to Kansas City. They wrote to each other for about a year before getting together again in LA. They started dating and just having fun. They were soon married and had a Catholic wedding in LA. My sister Connie was born in 1943 in Marysville, CA and two years later I came along.

I don't remember where they lived at the time, but Mom had insisted I be born in California, so she traveled there for my birth. She had fond memories of California all her life. The air was warm and clean and the skies were clear. She and Dad recalled smelling the orange blossoms in the air as they safely walked the streets of LA holding hands. Dad would frequently buy her an orchid corsage from a sidewalk vendor. The 1940s and 1950s were good times in this country.

My earliest recollection of our military life was living on a base in Tucson, Arizona as a little child and then moving to Munich, Germany for a few years. It was a ten-day trip by boat back then. While in Munich we had a housekeeper named Anna Lee, whose young son Johan didn't speak English. So, for the two-plus years we were there I learned to speak some German while playing with the little guy.

Then we returned to the states and relocated to Rome, New York, where my brother Mike was born. I was about nine years old at the time. While living there for about a year or so, Mom put me through Catholic Catechism indoctrination, called Confirmation, and then I partook in my First Holy Communion ceremony at the Catholic Church. I still have pictures of the event. I was wearing a white suit and held a Rosary draped over my praying hands. I didn't know much other than it was something I was supposed to do and was required by the church.

We were then transferred to Robins Air Force Base in Warner Robins, Georgia. There I was enrolled in a Catholic school where we were required to wear grey and white uniforms. At that time, I remember the church feeling hollow, cold, and empty, maybe a little "holy" but in a scary kind of way. My teacher was Sister Mary Ignatius, a strict bespectacled nun who didn't put up with any nonsense. It's funny the things we remember from the past. It was there at the school where another student showed me how to "flip the bird," otherwise called "giving the finger" (the middle finger, that is). I didn't know what it meant and just thought it was funny.

In the sixth grade, there was a new kid who had flunked the last three grades. He looked like a young man to me, mostly because he was about a foot taller than everyone else. His gig was bullying. Because of his age and size, he was an imposing figure. He used to sneak up and corner his victims and then punch them repeatedly until they either surrendered or broke away. I had been watching him fearfully every day, and then one day our eyes met. He saw me avoiding him and he started closing in. I ran home feeling fearful and angry inside. I was angry at him but mostly at myself. I told my mom what happened, and she told my dad (who had been a boxer in the Army) to teach me how to defend myself. I also remember finding some magazine articles on Jujitsu and analyzing the techniques and moves. Not long afterward, after continually watching my "six" and avoiding the bully, he appeared out of nowhere during a recess and said, "Got ya!"

He had me cornered and started moving in for the kill. At least that's what it felt like! Without warning, an emotion I had never felt before came over me. Like lightning, without any thought or plan, I attacked him. I jumped into his face, got him into a headlock, and threw him over my hip and onto the ground. I followed through by dropping my hip onto his abdomen, knocking the wind out of him. I then started to "ground and pound" the guy, punching him repeatedly, with alternating left and right blows as hard and fast as I could. I was dragged off him by a teacher who seemed to come out of nowhere, but not before I pounded the guy black and blue.

The bully was stunned. The teacher ordered us both to go directly to the principal's office. We dusted ourselves off and started walking toward the office when the big kid smiled and put his arm around my shoulder, respectfully hugging me as he said, "You're alright!" He said he never saw that coming, and honestly, neither did I.

That was my first taste of mad dog violence. It gave me confidence in myself and taught me I didn't have to submit to abuse or ridicule, and obviously, I could defend myself. Right then and there, I decided I would never again bow or submit to a physical threat. Instead, I would fight to win. After our scolding, I walked out of the principal's office with my head held high.

After finishing up at the Catholic school, I went to a secular Junior High. Once again, I was a little humbled by the size and aggressive nature of some of the students. Soon after starting, I was challenged by an older, bigger kid between classes. I mentally stood down, not wanting to fight, but when the guy took a step toward me, my lifelong friend Robert Morgan (rest in peace, my brother) stepped in and told the guy to pick on someone his size. Robert was two years older than me. When Robert assumed a Judo stance, the guy started to laugh at him, and Robert immediately took him down. Boom! It was over. End of fight. I was very impressed, not to mention grateful as well.

No matter where in the world we each lived, Robert and I remained close friends and brothers to the end. He passed away in 2021 from heart failure and I still feel a deep sense of loss. He was retired from the California Department of Fish and Game. He had been a pilot with the department and flew government dignitaries over land and lake projects, planting fish in the lakes, viewing and counting wildlife herds, and generally guiding tours. After retiring from the Sacramento area, he married a beautiful soulmate named Linda. They lived only thirty minutes away from me and my wife Reann when he went home to be with the Lord. The good news is he had also become a committed believer and follower of Jesus. We will one day be reunited in Heaven.

While living in Georgia I remember visiting my Grandparent's 80-acre farm in Hamler, Ohio. It was there I learned to shoot guns at around eight years of age. My Grampa had a single-shot shotgun and a couple of single-shot .22s. They were readily available and kept in a little storage area in the "mud room" at the back entryway. One was a Remington "rolling block" and the other was a Stevens "falling block" action. I was soon turned loose after a demonstration and safety training by my dad. He showed me how the bullet goes where the barrel is pointed and to never point it at a person, ever. He shot a tin can to show me how the little .22 Rimfire could penetrate both sides of a can, meaning it was, in fact, a deadly weapon. I was given the okay to hunt the farm's eighty acres and shoot a light birdshot load in the granary, which was a haven for sparrows.

On one trip to stay with Gramma and Grampa, I was introduced to a kid from a neighboring farm. Our parents thought we should hang out and keep each other company. Meanwhile, Mom and Dad could visit with my dad's folks. I had never hunted with anyone but myself back then. This kid and I both liked guns and we were soon turned loose on the farm to take on the ever-present sparrow flocks. We decided to climb up into the hayloft of Grampa's barn. As we sat there, we readied our guns and loaded them up. We were using .22 Rimfire birdshot. The sparrows were used to flying into the hayloft through the second-level loft-door opening. We got a few shots off but then the action slowed.

All was quiet, but then I felt the kid quietly staring at me. I did a double take because he was pointing his rifle at me with a maniacal look on his face. I didn't know if he had a round in the chamber or not. I told him to stop pointing his gun at me, but he said nothing and persisted. I knew we were using birdshot instead of regular bullets but for all I knew he may have had some regular loads on him. I felt sure I was about to be shot. So, I told the kid to watch me very carefully. I then opened the action on my single-shot rifle and held up a cartridge for him to see. Then I put it in the chamber, cocked the hammer and I pointed it right between his eyes from about five feet away (sorry, Dad). That freaked him out and he put his gun down and said, "Okay, okay!" I told him I was done hunting with him and sent him down the road. I never wanted to see him again.

As I write this, I realize how ever since I came to true faith I can no longer hunt or kill anything again (except for food in a survival crisis). All life is precious to me. However, I am a sheepdog and not a sheep and will defend a life without hesitation if one is in danger of death or great bodily harm.

2

ROME

AFTER ALMOST SIX years in Georgia, my dad got a dream assignment at Ciampino Airport in Rome, Italy. It was a joint civilian airport and U.S. Air Force installation at the time. The year was 1959. To me, there was no culture shock, just fun and exciting things to see and do. The history on display everywhere I looked was incredibly exciting!

My new high school was international in nature, secular, and named the Overseas School of Rome or OSR. We had kids there from many countries of the United Nations. Fortunately for me, it was an English-speaking school. However, it wasn't long before I began communicating quite well with the locals and even became aware of the many slang words and dialects used in different areas.

Of course, as a new freshman beginning in the middle of the school year, it wasn't long before I again needed to call upon the lessons and skills I had acquired in Georgia. Soon after I started classes, we had a basketball game going on the outside court in which I was picked as captain for my side. The opposing team's captain was a Lebanese guy. He was a junior and I was the new freshman kid. Here we go again! I remember him being about my size. He had a very dark five o'clock shadow and looked very mature and manly for a high school junior.

As the game started, the other team seemed as if they had no clue about basketball being a non-contact sport. After a few serious fouls, I called for him to control his team. He took this as a personal challenge and tried to get in my face. I again asked him to just stop the continual and intentional fouls on his side. He became offended and started threatening to hit me. Finally, seeing things were going nowhere, I told him if it would make him feel better, I would give him the first punch. He chose to punch me in the shoulder, putting some gusto into it. I smiled at him and said, "That's it?"

He then wound up and hit me again as hard as he could. Oops, that tripped my switch, and I went into survival mode. I took him down hard and pounded his face until a teacher pulled me off. The next day at school the guy showed up looking like he had been hit by a bus. Frankly, I was shocked! He had lumps on his head, both eyes were black and blue and tightly swollen. His lips were split in three places and swollen up like bananas. I couldn't believe he even came to school looking as bad as he did. I had come out of it without a mark on me.

As soon as he saw me in the hallway between classes, he again challenged me. He was extremely serious and wanted to go another round. Was this guy nuts or what? I refused and told him I would hurt him worse if he didn't leave me alone. Again, a teacher intervened, but not before the kid could show me the knife scars on his neck from fights in his country. This kid was hardcore. Fortunately, after that, he never bothered me again. I wonder where he ended up in life. Thinking about it today, he was possible terrorist material. I was becoming more aware of some of the cultural differences between countries and how they think and interact.

While in Rome for the next three-and-a-half years, I learned to communicate well and enjoyed the freedom knowing different languages allows. In school I studied French, which was helpful when we toured Europe, and although I knew very little, I knew enough. I had some German, quite a bit of Italian, and Croatian (mostly

Rome

colorful words Mom would spew out when she was mad at us kids). I'm certain her brutal upbringing had a lot to do with that. She never hit us, but when we pushed her buttons, she would pound on the kitchen counter and start cursing in Croatian. When this happened, we would quickly vacate the room and sometimes the house. When she was about eighty years old, she got on her knees with my sister Connie and gave her heart to Jesus. As the years passed, I witnessed a softness come over Mom. She did a complete 180.

While in Europe we toured all over, hitting mostly western European countries from Italy to England. Everything was so exciting: ancient structures, cobblestone streets, castles, and monasteries. We even visited the grave of my great grandfather in Ogulin, Yugoslavia (Croatia). There was only one gas pump in the tiny town, and you had to siphon-pump it with a hand-lever. We ate farm-raised food in the little house my great grandfather was born in. It still had its original dirt floor. They also made homemade strudel for us, and I ate so much I got sick.

The only sports we had in high school in Rome were gymnastics and basketball, and I made the first-string varsity team and played throughout my high school years. We would compete against other schools and travel by train at times with the cheerleaders and several school chaperones. Looking back, I'm not sure who was chaperoning who!

When we first got to Rome, my dad bought me a used motorbike to putt around on. It was a little 50cc bike with a centrifugal clutch. It started by first pedaling it like a bicycle and when the motor started sputtering all you had to do was twist the throttle and you were off and running. During my high school years, I was continually on two wheels. If I wasn't on my motorbike, then I was on a rented Vespa or Lambretta. We lived in the hills south of Rome in a little town named Grottaferatta. It took less than thirty minutes to get from Rome to our two-story Italian villa in the hills.

Whenever I got stuck in Rome at night without a ride, I would walk around until I found a motorcycle with a key in it, crank it up, and ride the twenty miles home. I would then park it several blocks from our villa and the "policia" would get it back to the owner. I know this because one time I "borrowed" the same bike *again* from the same street in Rome. The owner must have been a slow learner!

In Italy in the 1960s, there was no minimum age for drinking alcohol. There were no drugs in our school, or at least none I ever saw or even heard about. We kids would hit the pizza parlors and order pitchers of beer with our pizzas. In three-and-a-half years I only remember seeing one staggering drunk Italian on the streets. There had to be more, but I never saw them. My life was consumed with riding my motorbike, chasing girls, drinking beer, and shooting hoops. I remember reading little paperback books about bikers and motorcycles. I loved the look of Levis, white T-shirts (with a pack of Lucky Strikes rolled up in a sleeve), and black engineer boots with the buckle across the top. Our school wouldn't let us dress like that, but I admired the look and was drawn to the lifestyle. My heart identified with the rebels in the little pocket novels.

I barely graduated from high school. My grades were truly deplorable (a humorously overused adjective now, thanks to Hillary Clinton's references to the Republicans in her 2016 Presidential campaign). But I made it through by the grace of God and a compassionate teacher who decided at the last moment to give me a passing grade. It was that close!

3
BACK TO THE HOMELAND

AFTER RETURNING TO the states in 1963, the family moved to Hershey, Pennsylvania and then to San Luis Obispo, California a year later. It is one of the most beautiful places in the United States. By then Dad had retired from the Air Force as a Lt. Colonel. When my folks decided to move back east again for Dad's new civil service job in Maryland, I stayed in California. I loved the weather, the girls, the beaches, the hotrods, and the custom choppers. Not knowing what to do with my future, I got a job in construction working on a new golf course, first with ground-up construction and later in the pro shop.

I remember learning how to run a Caterpillar tractor and a backhoe. One day I needed to hop a ride on a road grader. It looked like a huge praying mantis. The tires were taller than me. As I got up into the passenger seat next to the operator, I noticed a large coil of half-inch steel cable on the floorboards. I had nowhere to put my feet but on top of it. As we took off on the main road, our speed was building up.

Then I heard a strange sound and felt a vibration under my feet. Someone had left an end of the cable hanging down from the right side of the grader, dangling close to one of the huge wheels. As our speed increased the cable swung back and was caught up by a heavy rear tire. One of the coils my feet were on had pulled up and caught both my ankles, dragging my feet over to a four-inch lip on the right side of the floorboards. The lip was designed to keep your feet inside the seating area. I couldn't kick free of it. The operator heard the noise of the sizzling steel cable as it became wrapped around the rear wheel.

It was incredibly noisy up top where we were seated, and I was screaming at the top of my lungs for the driver to stop. That type of heavy machinery doesn't stop very fast. The driver slammed on the brakes as the cables gripped me like a python crushing a rodent. When we came to a stop, I was trapped. The driver quickly put it in reverse and slowly backed up allowing the cable to loosen its death grip on my booted ankles. Had we gone another couple of feet I would be wearing prosthetics today, assuming I wouldn't have bled to death first. The cable loop had cut through the outer leather of my boot tops, but miraculously I was unscathed. I was back to work the next day as if nothing happened. Ah, the resilience of youth!

When the rains came, we kept on working as much as the weather would permit. During a break in the weather, the construction manager who taught me to operate a Cat told me to get the backhoe tractor parked nearby so he could teach me how to use it. I got on it, fired it up, and drove it over to a little sidehill. He had me set it up facing a certain direction so I could start digging a trench for a large waterline.

There were stout hydraulic stabilizer legs to help support the top-heavy machine. I learned how things worked and the manager was satisfied I was doing well. He gave me a thumbs up and walked off to another worker on the site. As I started digging the trench, I would have to move the rig a little at a time and re-stabilize the backhoe. One time when I got re-established, I was at a slight side angle. But with the lay of the land, I did what I had to do to finish my assignment.

Several things were working against me at the time. The ground was wet and muddy. As I put the stabilizers down, one of my rear wheels came a little off the ground and started spinning. Before I knew it the whole machine started to tip over. The spinning wheel was on my left side close to my knee. As the machine started shifting in the mud it started tipping more to my left. I instinctively slid my foot over in that direction as you would if trying to stabilize your balance. Of course, it was impossible to avert the roll by doing so.

Remember the four-inch lip on the road grader that almost cost me both feet? Well, the backhoe didn't have such a lip, and my muddy foot slipped right off the floorboards and the spinning wheel grabbed my left leg and was pulling me down between the inside of the wheel and the frame of the tractor. In a panic, I kicked my leg forward and broke free from the grasp of the heavy tire tread. Somehow, I reached the kill switch and shut it down. As I sat atop the teetering machine, I slowly and carefully climbed off on the right side and jumped to the ground, again unscathed.

When the construction was complete, I was quite content to work in sales at the pro shop. Around the same time, I decided to enroll at Cuesta College, a public community college near San Luis Obispo, since everyone I knew was going there. I also got a job at a local Chevron station where I pumped gas, changed tires, and did oil changes. The high side of this job was having the perfect place to work on my '57 Chevy hotrod in the evenings.

While at Cuesta I decided to major in Social Science until I could figure out where life was taking me. It was there I met my first wife, Jane. My best friend, Bill Bowers was dating her twin sister, Jean. We had great times together, going to the drag races, cruising the main strip in town, and drinking beer at the drive-in theater. Those were carefree days.

After graduating from Cuesta College, I went on to Cal Poly University in San Luis Obispo where I attended part-time for two years. It is located only ten miles as the crow flies from the gorgeous central California coast. I had one more year to go at Cal Poly but never finished. I moved on to other endeavors, always seeking excitement, my place in life, and peace for my soul.

4

Fast Forward

Enough about my formative years. Fast forward now to the 1980s. I had been married and divorced twice by then. My second wife, Dianne, worked at an upper-class department store, in the ladies' section. She was a party girl and liked to have fun. She was a good wife, but our differences eventually pulled us apart. We parted on good terms and moved on with our lives.

The crowd I had been running with liked to drink and party. Those were different times, and it seemed everyone I knew was prone to the "fast life." I struggled with pride, selfishness, and the lusts of the world. I would think at times, "Is this all there is?"

I had guilt over my first divorce, both for hurting my wife and for leaving our son, Ryan, without a father. After his birth, Jane soon became pregnant with our second child. I selfishly felt it was too soon to have another child and so we decided to get an abortion. I have never forgotten such a horrible mistake. How do you shake that kind of guilt? As you can see, I had some baggage and no one to blame but myself. Life can be a serious learning curve for some of us!

By this time, I had been a student, worked in construction running heavy equipment, tied steel for concrete foundations, and did some roofing. I also worked at a high-end body shop for a little while. For my hobby, I put in years working out at local gyms until my biceps measured over nineteen inches. I had stretched out my college by going part-time and taking classes here and there. Truth be told, my muscles were growing faster than my intellect.

I was always interested in fast cars and motorcycles. Off and on I would take one of my car projects down to the Santa Maria dragstrip and race. For a while, I had a turbocharged Chevy Corvair convertible, of all things. I decided to insulate the exhaust intake going into the turbocharger, an idea I saw in *Hot Rod* magazine. Holy Cow! What a difference this made when the turbo kicked in. I was unbeatable in my class. It was just small-time fun stuff. I was still looking for a purpose in life, but as usual in all the wrong places.

In 1980 I met a man named Guy Hogue and we became good friends. He was a highly skilled craftsman. He was running a small business making custom pistol grips out of exotic hardwoods in a little shop at his home in Cambria, California.

Guy taught me the trade and I had a lot of fun with it, eventually making pistol grips out of my garage for extra money. One day he called me up and said he had invented a new way of attaching a pistol grip to a revolver. He obtained a patent on his idea and asked a gun-writer named James Mason and me to partner with him to mass produce and market his product.

We became incorporated and I was asked to set up a network of dealer reps to sell the products to dealers. Guy Hogue did all the research and development work and Jim Mason was to promote the grips through advertising and writing product reviews in the gun magazines. We all did our best and got the brand on the map. Before long, we were all driving leased BMWs. When we incorporated the business, we had been warned by our attorney from the very beginning how partnerships have a high failure rate, and to be aware we could run into troubles down the road. And that's exactly what happened.

Guy had lost his wife, the mother of their three boys, in a horrific accident. A powerline had fallen onto their neighbor's property and the owner's wife was trying to put out a small fire it had started. While doing so, she accidentally touched the line and was being electrocuted. Guy's wife, Jill, was standing near to her and tried to push her free from the line. It worked and broke the woman free from the shock. But in the process, Jill came into contact with the powerline and took the hit.

Guy ran to her aid but was knocked back by the voltage three times as he tried to pull her free. He told me after his third attempt her body started smoking and turning black. He knew his soulmate was gone. One of his sons who was there also witnessed the tragedy. He said he took his son by the hand and simply walked away. I knew Guy's wife and she was a truly sweet Christian lady.

Guy was a dear friend and I loved him like a brother. He had taught me his trade and put a lot of heart into our relationship. But eventually, just as our attorney had warned, we began getting into disagreements. We were all working from separate locations which eventually made communications challenging and frustrating. After several years, James and I sold our shares to Guy, and we all went our separate ways.

The story ended well for the Hogue family. After Guy passed away, his oldest son Aaron, with the help of his brother Patrick, went on to build a hugely successful business in the firearms industry. His other brother Kenny also worked at the company for a while. These days, some of the current department heads have their own airplanes, forming what people call the "Hogue Air Force." Guy would be quite proud. At one time he talked with me about his faith (that was before I knew Jesus). I believe he is now rejoicing in Heaven with his sweet wife.

There I was again, back to square one, wondering what to do next. After much thought, I decided to pursue a lifelong interest in horses. As a kid I faithfully watched all the Roy Rogers and Lone Ranger episodes on TV and loved all the John Wayne westerns. I guess I was always a cowboy at heart.

By this time my brother Mike had been a rodeo cowboy for a number of years and I admired the freewheeling independent lifestyle. I had even ridden a bull once just to see what it was like. I already owned a horse and a trailer and had purchased a new house on a one-acre lot in the little town of Santa Margarita. I started going to all the top "training clinics" with famous trainers such as Tom Dorrance, Ray Hunt, and Pat Pirelli. This led to a job at the Pirelli Horse Ranch in Stockton, California, about four hours to the north of me. I used to sleep on the office couch during the week and would return home on weekends.

I became deeply immersed in animal psychology and communication through kinesics (nonverbal communication through body movements). It was a gentle method of breaking horses—only we didn't "break" them, we trained them to become willing and harmonious partners. We learned their language (so to speak) by simply making the right thing easy and the wrong thing difficult. Then we would observe, remember, and compare. Once the horse "got it," then the right thing became their first choice. When done correctly, it was like two dancers, one leading and the other smoothly following. Working with unbroken, wild, and "problem horses" became my specialty. It always turned out that those "problem" horses, in reality, had problem owners, not the other way around.

I had built a round corral for training and set up metal fenced paddocks for my customers' horses. Bordering my property were thousands of acres of ranch land to ride on. With all this and a previous worker's compensation settlement from a miscellaneous work injury, I was making out quite well for the times. I continued my work with horses for about six years.

I would have Ryan on the weekends, and he really liked riding horses with me and my brother, his Uncle Mike. We would trailer out to Montana De Oro state park, east of nearby Los Osos. There were miles and miles of sandy trails leading through the hills to cliffs overlooking the Pacific Ocean. Those were great times for a father and son to have fun, bond, and just be together, even though we lived apart.

On the side I was still going to the gym continually, but I had also begun writing cowboy poetry. Before long, Mike and I started going to the annual Cowboy Poetry Gathering in Elko, Nevada to watch the pros perform. There we met Ramblin' Jack Elliot, famous folk and country-western singer and songwriter. We immediately became good friends. In the coming years he would visit us in his motorhome, ride horses with us, and "sing for his supper." We would get a little tipsy and have a blast.

While visiting Elko one year I met some of the folks from *Western Horsemen* magazine. After I shared a little bit about my work with horses, they asked if I would like to write an article for them about what I do and how I do it. The method I had learned involved using a commonsense psychological approach, and the magazine wanted to share the technique with their readers. As I mentioned above, I had simply learned to communicate my will and dominance to the horse I was working with.

Just to cover my bases I submitted two articles in case they didn't like one or the other. They bought them both, complete with pictures, which led to a run of dozens of published articles. I was gifted with an analytical mind and the ability to put my thoughts and techniques into words. I had several poems published as well during that time. It seemed as if I was on a roll, and I was having a lot of fun with it.

On yet another trip to Elko, Mike and I were approached by a guy who introduced himself as Christopher Coppola, the son of the famous filmmaker, Francis Ford Coppola. Christopher is a half-brother to famous actor Nicolas Cage. He asked if we would like to audition for a part in a western movie he was making. I thought it was a little unusual and tried to laugh it off, but he was persistent and asked us to meet him and his audition crew who were set up at a local saloon in downtown Elko.

During some small talk, he asked me if I knew anything about guns, especially western cowboy-type guns. I told him I did and how I got my first single action six-gun when I was just fourteen years old. I had learned back then how to do "fast draw" and gun spinning tricks. Guns had been a longtime hobby and I had also been a competitive shooter for several years and had the trophies to prove it. This piqued his interest even more.

Mike and I did a lot of things together in those days. He helped me with the horse training and is credited for taking most of the pictures published in my training articles. On a whim, we went to the audition. Mike and I read the lines as directed and then went back to enjoying all the fun, friends, and people at the gathering. We even met the famous cowboy poet Baxter Black. He shared some words of wisdom with us I have never forgotten. They apply to so many things in life. He said, "Do you know the difference between good poetry and bad poetry?" He then said one word: "Laziness." Thanks, Baxie (RIP)!

When we returned home from Elko, I continued my work with horses, and about a week later got a call from an LA producer who offered me a co-starring role as "Tex" the villain in Coppola's upcoming film. He said that while screening all the auditions,

Francis Ford Coppola pointed to me on the screen and said, "There's your villain," and that was that! Again, I tried to blow it off, but persistence won out as the producer assured me this was the real deal. He soon sent me the script and a contract. Are you kidding me? Was this really happening? I was no actor! Nonetheless, I decided to give it a try if just for the fun and experience. After all, it was a co-starring role! How often does something like this happen to a guy?

I soon found myself in a guest cabin on a ranch near Elko preparing for the next six weeks of filming on location. The movie was titled *Gunfighter*. The first person I met at the cabin was Clu Gulager, an actor originally of black and white television fame. He had been one of my childhood heroes starring in a series called *Billy the Kid*. He has also acted in countless movies over the decades. Pro-Rodeo Hall of Famer "Chris Lybbert" starred as the hero of the film. An "extra" in the film was Don Farmer, a former 1972 Saddle Bronc Riding Champion. Don is now a famous western artist and has won many art awards. His work is amazing.

The new western had a very low $100,000 budget, which I heard expanded to over $1,000,000 by the time of completion. From the beginning, the purpose of the project was to use mostly non-union people with no acting experience to make a fun western movie with a ridiculously low budget. There were also cameo roles filled by bigger names such as Martin Sheen and Robert Carradine. It was never a hit, but I wouldn't trade the experience for anything. I made some new friends and met a few legends. I was pumped about the fun of the work, so when I returned home, I found a local acting agency to find me other acting opportunities.

I soon auditioned for the part of a uniformed street cop with only two lines in a movie called *No Place to Run*. It was a Hollywood union movie co-starring Mark Hamill of *Star Wars* fame, and I gladly signed on. I had to hang around the set for two days until I was called. My actual work took about an hour and a half for which I was paid $1,600. It was a union movie, and by getting a speaking role I could apply for membership in the Screen Actors Guild. By then we were into the 1990s.

Next came a non-speaking role in *Arachnophobia*. It appeared I was going backward instead of forward. I did a few commercials after that and then things just fizzled out. To do it right I was told I needed to move to LA and do weekly auditions. I just wasn't willing to leave what we call "God's Country" here on the central Cali coast.

After my microscopic acting career (under another name) I became a hunting guide up in Wyoming for a couple of seasons. I had hunted all my life, taking over forty-head of big game. Brother Mike had started a professional guiding business up there and I was just filling in for a while.

On one of the Wyoming hunts, we were guiding for deer and antelope. One of the hunters had a doe tag he wanted to fill for freezer meat. The hills were full of antelope herds and finding a nice fat doe would be a simple matter. As we came up over a rise, we spotted a small herd grazing. I quickly got the hunter set up for a shot. The distance was less than 150 yards. When he fired, the doe was hit in the gut. The rest of the herd began running off. But the doe couldn't move. Her intestines were spilling out and she was bleating in pain. The alpha buck left the herd and returned to get the doe. When he got to her, he used his horns to try to keep her on her feet, but she kept bleating loudly and trying to lay down.

After she laid down the buck kept trying to get her back up. A couple of the hunters started laughing. It broke my heart. A second shot boomed across the valley and the doe's head dropped to the ground. As we approached the downed antelope, the buck was still hanging back from his herd, obviously stressing over the doe. He watched from a distance and then when it was over, he turned and rejoined the herd.

After killing the doe, the hunters cheered and secured their weapons. One of them cracked open a bottle of rum and passed it around to celebrate the kill. I passed. For me, this pretty much ended any desire to ever kill another animal ever again. I was becoming a different person and began thinking more about God and all His beautiful creations. Death can be so ugly! I came to realize how I was changing and becoming more compassionate. Maybe God had a plan for my life, but I wasn't "there" yet.

While training horses I came to know my third wife, Lorrie. She was an endurance horse racer who competed in 100-mile cross country races. Our life together fizzled out within about three years. There were too many obstacles, such as her suddenly wanting to have a baby when I didn't. Before we got married, we had both agreed not to have any children. I could see the writing on the wall. After that, she hooked up with a cowboy down the road and asked me for a divorce. She had kept her cowboy friend on a backburner and after our divorce, they soon married. There were lots of miles, lots of trials! Life sure ain't for sissies!

A number of years later, Reann became my fourth wife. We had known each other for many years prior. We dated off and on for a while, but I had failed at marriage so many times I just couldn't commit to a serious relationship, let alone another marriage. We had many interests in common. We toured the northwestern states together, and we were both gym rats and loved the same movies and music. But the nexus that cinched the deal was faith-based. We both came to Christ separately during some time apart.

I had prayed long and hard about having another woman in my life. I strongly felt if I ever married again, I would need the Lord's leading and direction. I was struggling with a great deal of back pain at the time. Out of the blue I got a call from Reann and she offered to come over to clean the house and cook me a meal. She emphasized, "No strings attached." I could hardly walk at the time and needed the help.

God reconnected us, and we were soon baptized together in the Pacific Ocean at Cayucos, California. She was truly a Godsend! We lived separately and remained celibate until united by marriage a year later. I don't know what I would do without her!

5
SPEAKING OF GOD!

BEFORE MY MARRIAGE to Reann, I had rented a room from my mom at the family home my dad had built back in the mid-1980s after he finally retired for good. Dad had passed away by that time, Mom was lonely, and I needed a roof over my head. I had quit the horse business by then and it just worked out for us both.

While renting with Mom, I started shooting again. I had developed a keen interest in long-range shooting and purchased three ballistics software programs for my computer. Before long, I had a cool ballistics consulting business that kept the wolves from the door over the next two decades. I was just living life, with no debts and no responsibilities.

That summer my sister Connie came out for a visit from Virginia where she was working in high-dollar real estate. There had been some tension between Connie and me for a while, just a little family baggage. But this time, in the summer of 1998, it was different. I had been feeling God was drawing me closer to Him. I kept thinking I was missing something important in my life. I had a new truck, no debts, a good income, and not a care in the world. So, what was missing? All the "feel good" things had simply become fleeting, temporary fixes.

One day while visiting on the back porch, Connie offered me a little Billy Graham tract. I accepted it and that evening I noticed it on the nightstand by my bed. I hesitated, but then picked it up. It showed a sketch of a person standing on one side of a huge chasm and the word "God" on the other. It asked, how do we get to the other side to be with God? When I turned the page, I saw a big cross connecting the two sides and a person walking across it toward God. The little booklet was only a few pages, but it was so simple even a young child could understand it.

I remember asking myself why I was feeling hesitant about praying the prayer in the tract, asking the Lord into my heart. I shamefully asked myself what it was going to cost me, as in what would I have to give up? I thought about sex outside of marriage (I was single at the time). And what about cussing (real men cuss, right?), and how about drinking? I had been a drinker all my life. Most baby boomers come from an era where drinking and smoking were the norm. Thankfully, I had already quit smoking years before.

I began thinking how I knew it wasn't good to take the Lord's name in vain. I knew it was disrespectful and I felt in my spirit I needed to stop doing it immediately. Then I thought about my language around men. In the secular world, men cuss. They always have. But I began to think if it was offensive to God then it would be a no-brainer to give it up. I realized how using rude and crude language honestly sounded ignorant to me. I also realized how most of the world couldn't care less whether I cussed or not. I decided right then I would never use obscene gestures or cuss again. I didn't need it, and God was more important. I needed His approval, not anyone else's.

As for celibacy, I was willing to try my best (and I succeeded). This left me with one other concern: drinking. I was never into street drugs, but alcohol had been my daily go-to for all my adult life. I had never been a sloppy, falling-down drunk. In fact, I was very functional on alcohol. It relaxed me, and in public settings it helped me to socialize. I drank heavier in my younger days but as I was getting a little older, I would drink about three, sometimes four beers a day, around four o'clock in the afternoon. Then on weekends I would drink a couple of beers and mix up some margaritas. It was a big part of my life. Over the decades of my adult years, I had tried many times to give it up, especially on days when I would wake up with a head-pounding hangover.

As I kept looking at the tract I started praying. I told the Lord if He wanted me to quit drinking then I would need His help. I was too weak. I recalled the days when I had poured all the alcohol in the house down the drain and then went out and bought some more the next day. It was a lifecycle of addiction. As I prayed, I felt God was calling me to Him. I told Him I was unworthy of His love and how I was a sinner. My fear was I would fail again and let Him down. But the calling was too strong to resist.

I told the Lord I was all in, but not without His mercy and help. I told Him from that day forward I was His. I said, "Lord, I messed up the first half of my life, but the last half is yours, so use me until you use me up, then beam me up. I'm yours." I also asked Him to show me anything in my life that was displeasing to Him. Then I prayed the little prayer inside the booklet and this simple step of faith impacted my whole life. My eyes and ears were opened to discern the truth! I felt like a huge weight had been lifted off my shoulders. I was at peace as I turned off the light and fell asleep.

Connie asked me the next day if I had read the tract she had given me and I told her I had. She asked if I prayed the prayer inside and if so, did I mean it? I told her yes to both questions and how I had done so to the best of my ability. She was so excited! She went right out and bought me a New King James student version Bible. She had me start with the Gospel of John and there was no looking back! I read that "In the beginning was the Word, and the Word was with God, and the Word was God...and the Word became flesh and dwelt among us" (John 1:1, 14, NKJV). Those words hit me like a ton of bricks! From that moment on I knew it was all true. I was given a glimpse of faith and I devoured it like a rabid dog. I couldn't put the Bible down.

The day after I asked God to help me quit drinking, I went to the fridge at my usual time and reached for a beer. My, what a short memory! Then I realized I had just asked God in prayer to help me quit. Then I heard a humorous voice in my head say, "Close the door, fool." Aww man, I thought! But I closed the door. This time I had left all the alcohol in the house right where it was. The scene at the refrigerator repeated itself day after day. "Close the door, fool!"

The next thing I knew a month had gone by. But I dared to say to the Lord, since I had gone a month and had proven myself, would it be okay if I just had a beer now and then? "Close the door, fool!" So, I did. Then a year rolled around and again I felt I had proven myself. So again, I asked the Lord if I could just have one, to which I heard in my spirit, "Do you want to waste the last year?" In reply, I said "No!" Then after the two-year mark I had to ask myself, "Do I want to waste the last two years?" Heck no! I was done.

It was then that I poured all the old booze down the drain and never looked back. That was more than twenty-four years ago, and I have never had a drink since asking the Lord for His help. No AA, no NA, just Jesus. He is forever faithful!

After joining a local church and reading the Bible cover to cover, I was completely sold on my newfound Christian faith. Over the next several years I read five different versions of the Bible. What I wanted next was to find a ministry to challenge a guy like me.

6

Harley Davidson

I DIDN'T MAKE the connection at the time, but I began to think about motorcycles for some reason. I would sit in Mom and Dad's old house, which by then I had bought, and I would hear sounds from the freeway less than a half-mile away. It was summertime and I was hearing the roar of Harleys droning in the distance. The sound resonated down the chimney of the huge "walk-in" fireplace in the living room.

I began thinking of my younger years in the 1970s and how I had bought a "basket-case" Norton Commando 750 Twin and got it running. I remembered one cold, dark moonless night riding home. It was only a ten-mile ride. As I was sailing along, the front end of the bike started getting squirrely, like I had hit some ice. But it wasn't ice. My front tire had gone flat. I kept the bike nice and straight and stayed off the front brake. The more I slowed down the "squirrelier" it got. I was on a narrow two-lane country road, so I rode it out and got as close to the shoulder as I could to avoid being hit from behind.

As I was almost stopped, I was pleased with myself for avoiding a fall. But as I put both feet out to balance the bike, there was no foothold for my right foot because I was on the very edge of a drainage ditch. As the bike teetered to the right, down I went, into the drainage ditch, which was filled with water. The bike came sliding down with me, pinning my right leg under the bike. Not only that, but the throttle kicked wide open and the bike was still in gear, which left the rear wheel spinning wildly as I lay there in the cold dark water with the bike on top of me.

As the engine screamed out of control, I grappled for the kill switch. Finding it, I shut it down. As I dragged my leg out from under the bike, I couldn't believe what had just happened. But I sucked it up, knowing I needed to get myself as well as my bike out of the ditch. And, of course, when I needed help there wasn't another vehicle on the road. I pushed and pulled, making headway an inch at a time, lifting and dragging the front wheel and then the back, back and forth, up the muddy embankment until I got it up and onto the edge of the road where I could put the kickstand down.

I was muddy, wet, and cold, but I was unharmed. I left the bike where it was and started walking home until finally a car came by and gave me a lift. The next day I got the wheel off and the tire repaired, tightened her up, and was happily back in the wind. When you're young, you just take things in stride and carry on.

As the sound of motors echoed down my chimney, I also thought about my old Bultaco 250cc dirt bike. After my son Ryan came into my life, I remember giving him rides on the gas tank and how much fun we had. As I continued reminiscing, I also thought about how I was getting older and had never gotten a Harley. I always wanted one.

I had already been sharing my newfound faith with many people I would meet here and there. As I continued to pray for a ministry, one day I found myself standing in the crowded showroom of Gary Bang's Harley Davidson in Atascadero. I was a little nervous and didn't know what I was looking for. There were big touring models, medium-size models, and smaller Sportster models. My heart settled on a brand new 2001 Low Rider. It was a medium size and looked about right. It was hot metallic orange and vivid black with gleaming chrome accents.

When I walked out, I had a sales receipt in my hand for over $18,000. I asked them to deliver the bike to the house, which they did immediately. Gary Bang himself (now a Harley Davidson Hall of Famer) followed me home on the bike and I took him back to the shop in my Jeep. I thought, "Holy Cow, I just bought a Harley!" I was nervous about the price and hadn't ridden in a long time, but I was absolutely in love. It was a head-turning, blindingly stunning bike.

I thought the new bike was well deserved and a good way to enjoy life. As I rode it around, I soon discovered how it was a people magnet. Every time I parked it, somebody would stop and say, "Beautiful bike, man." I found myself giving God the glory for the bike by always working Him into the conversation. But then I started feeling guilty and began thinking maybe I had brought an idol into my life and blew a lot of money in the process. I didn't know at the time how the enemy of our soul works against us. I was also clueless about what was happening to me and where I was headed.

As I struggled with guilt, I began to wonder how to connect with other Harley enthusiasts. I soon found out there was a local HOG (Harley Owners Group) chapter right there in town. I began to attend meetings, joined up, and started going on Harley runs. I began to feel like this would be a good place to share my faith a little. So, I approached it gently but boldly and found no resistance from anyone. I ended up being voted in as the new road captain for the group and started planning and leading the runs.

On one of them, I met a girl named Sandy. She was married to one of our members. Her husband was unable to go on this run, and I ended up visiting with her at a gas stop along the way. I remember sharing my faith with her and her being very polite and receptive. She was a real sweetheart and very popular. Not long afterward she was diagnosed with cancer and died within a month. Everyone was in shock and heartbroken. Before she died, I had sent her a little laminated prayer card I created with some scriptures from the Bible's book of Romans and the sinner's prayer of faith. I put it in a card with a personal note.

Our chapter and those closest to Sandy had done a little hospital run and gathered at her bedside with the hope of cheering her up a little when she was sick. For all we knew it might be the last time we would ever see her, which turned out to be the case. We never saw Sandy again. After her memorial service, her husband acknowledged how she got the card I sent and thanked me for what I had written inside. It was very sad.

After Sandy passed, I was unexpectedly asked by our chapter president to speak to the group because many of the members were distraught over her death. Before I could even think about it, I said yes. I must confess, up until this time I had a great fear of public speaking. I would rather have jumped on a slow boat to China to avoid it at all costs, and I'm not kidding! I went home and started praying, "Oh Lord what have I done?" I didn't know how I was going to handle the situation.

As I prayed, I thought about what Jesus had done for me and what a wuss I was being. As I prayed, I told the Lord, "I am willing to make a fool of myself for you. You're the only thing that matters and I should count it a privilege." I spent several days thinking and praying about it. I decided to keep my remarks to about ten minutes. As I carefully made out my notes, I delivered my first practice speech to a blank television screen in my living room. I remember thinking to myself how it wouldn't be that bad as there would probably only be about twenty or thirty people there and I'd know them all. No big deal, right?

Our meetings were always held in the back conference room of a local restaurant. When I got there, I nervously picked a spot to sit. The friends and chapter members began filtering in and soon there must have been a hundred people there! At least that's what it seemed like as the room kept filling up. Many of them I had never seen before. I felt flushed and fearful, like an oppressive weight I couldn't bear. I wasn't counting on so many people. Then I just hung my head in silent prayer, put a smile on my face, and repeated, "Lord, I am willing."

The president of the chapter took care of a little business and then announced me. I went forward, notes in hand. A calm came over me as I had never experienced before in times of severe stress. I began to speak, and the words just flowed like honey. I told everyone I was there to remember Sandy and to give them a message from her. I told them their beloved Sandy would want them to know exactly what the truth was and how she had been in the presence of Jesus. I told them Sandy would want to share the message of salvation with them and tell them it was a personal choice with eternal consequences.

The words came forth so smoothly I could hardly believe it was me speaking. I told them how the Bible tells us there is only one true God and our salvation comes from belief and faith in Him alone, through God's grace and our faith, not just by being a good person. I said Sandy wanted everyone to know how much she loves them and can't wait to reunite with them in Heaven. I told them Sandy knows the truth now and the message was crystal clear. If God *isn't* real and yet we have believed in Him, what have we lost? Nothing. But if He *is* real and we have not put our faith in Him, then we have lost our eternity in Heaven with the Lord and will be forever alone in torment and eternal darkness.

I went on to briefly tell them about the deep conversation I had with Sandy on our last chapter run. I told them when I heard how sick she was I sent her the message of salvation and the sinner's prayer in a get-well card. I let them know how I chose to believe Sandy had prayed the prayer and asked the Lord into her heart before she passed away. Also, I told them the Bible assures us that all who are saved will be reunited with their friends and family in Heaven. I told them it was a no-brainer, at least for me. I said Sandy was in Heaven with the Lord and we who believe will all see her again.

As I ended with a little prayer, I realized I had barely looked at my notes once I got started. I watched as some big, burly, tatted-up bikers removed their glasses, wiping away tears. I realized then and there how something amazing had just happened and how I had been privileged to be a small part of it.

I guess you could say it was my first actual "test" by the Lord. Perhaps He simply wanted me to be the voice for His message. Afterward, I was complimented and encouraged by many in the audience. One listener had even surmised I was a pastor. Too funny! "Hardly," I told him. I felt so good inside, though. God had just given me a taste of what I now call "cookies from Heaven." I began to think maybe I could be an encourager for my friends in the group.

7
OFF TO STURGIS, SD

I ONLY KEPT the 2001 Low Rider for about six months and then sold it to a friend. I immediately moved up to a larger Harley model for more comfort on the road trips. Soon afterward I decided to make the pilgrimage to Sturgis, South Dakota for their annual biker rally. There were seven of us riding to the event, which draws in well over a half-million bikers. Our group consisted of mostly secular riders.

I remember sharing with Sonia, a pretty, young, registered nurse. She said she was saved but having trouble with her walk. I encouraged her to read her Bible and to get back to church. One of the guys, Ross, overheard our conversation and tried to intervene several times and make light of it. We stayed on track however and he ended up listening as well. Sonia was hungry for fellowship with another believer. We hit it off and it was uplifting for both of us.

On this trip, I shared with another pretty lady, Jenny, also a nurse. She said she had been raised in a Salvation Army family in the strictest of fashions. She even took her Bible with her on dates to keep her out of trouble. She was raised with fear and trembling of the wrath of the Lord, lest she sin and be cast into hell for all eternity. When she went to college, a professor rejected a paper she had written, telling her *his* views about God and spirituality. It was her way out, and she grasped at his views as surely being a better way.

I was saddened to hear this, yet I have learned it is a common occurrence in many institutions of higher learning today. Also, some well-meaning Christian parents browbeat their children into fear of God through fire and brimstone warnings and threats, sometimes forcing "manmade" religious views and legalistic interpretations of the Bible onto their children. As a result, some children learn only about the fear of God and not about His grace and love for each of us. Many turn away from faith as soon as they get out on their own. I have known many people who had rejected the God of their Christian upbringing and adopted "new age" beliefs. Satan must surely dance with glee over instances such as those. It is disturbing and heartbreaking to me.

I tried sharing the simple message of salvation with Jenny, but she no longer chose to believe Jesus is the only way to heaven (John 14:6, NASB). I continued to gently minister to her from time to time but saw no progress. Sonia, on the other hand, seemed excited about getting back in the groove and going to church again. When we returned home, she did just that.

Shortly after getting back from Sturgis, we had our annual California Mid-State Motorcycle Rally. Ross showed up with Sonia. He was going through a divorce and seemed to be sweet on her. Again, I got into a spiritual discussion with Sonia, and again Ross came up and tried to make light of our conversation and change the subject. But we stayed on track, and once again he chose to listen rather than walk away.

I later emailed Ross and asked if he wanted to go for a ride and have lunch. We rode out to Cholame, not far from where I lived. Over lunch, the topic of his impending divorce came up. I had been praying about letting the Spirit lead if I was supposed to share more with him. My personality inclined me to try to make it happen, but the Holy Spirit compelled me to be patient, compassionate, and gentle. I tested the waters and when I saw an opportunity, I gave him my testimony.

He listened politely and I had no idea of its effect at the time. He admitted he considered himself an agnostic. I later learned from my Pastor, Tom Farrell, how "Jesus doesn't believe in agnostics. You're either for Him or against Him!" I wish I had known that line before, but maybe it's better I didn't. Before we headed back, I gave Ross a little tract with the sinner's prayer.

About three weeks later he called me and said he couldn't get our conversation out of his head. He asked if he could go to church with me. I just about dropped the phone! He lived about an hour away. I invited him to come for dinner the following Saturday night and to stay over for church the next day. This gave us more time to talk, and I shared many things from the Bible with him.

We called Sonia and invited her to go to church with us too, and she accepted. After the Sunday service, we went out for breakfast together. We did this weekly for about a month, and one day I couldn't stand it any longer and I had to ask Ross where he was with his faith. He smiled and said he had prayed the sinner's prayer weeks ago. Ross had become a believer and Sonia was back in church. They continued to date and attend church together.

8

How about a Coffee?

One day, while still a member of the Atascadero HOG chapter, I got a call from a girl named Peggy telling me her boyfriend Don had left her and her life was in total turmoil. She was looking for information on an upcoming motorcycle rally and wanted to attend. She was asking for directions to the final destination of the run. As I was talking with her, I asked the Lord through an inner thought if perhaps this could be a person He had chosen for me to minister to. It had become my habit to pray for one person a day to share my faith with in some way, whether big or small. The Spirit gave me a nudge, so I asked Peggy if she wanted to be my passenger for the ride. I made sure she understood I was engaged to Reann and it was not to be a date, just transportation for her so she could participate in the event. She accepted (of course, I had cleared everything with Reann first).

On the day of the run, Peggy must have talked for three hours straight about her and Don's miseries. Afterward, I asked if she would like to have coffee with me at the local Starbucks. She agreed and after getting our coffees we sat outside along the sidewalk in front. She again continued her tale of woe. At this point, I stopped her and asked if she would let me talk for just ten minutes. She agreed and I offered her a better way. I made her an offer I hoped she couldn't refuse. It was an offer from God, through me. He put it on my heart and provided the words, all I did was speak them.

I told Peggy what Jesus had done for me and the peace and love He provides. I asked her if she wanted to have that in her life and she said yes, very much so. I then asked her if she would pray the sinner's prayer with me to ask Jesus into her heart, and again she said yes. She took her first step toward God right there in front of Starbucks. I was so happy for her, as well as for myself, for the opportunity to be used in such a way!

Afterward, Peggy told me she would like to go to church with me and Reann. We agreed to meet at our church on the following Sunday. Don returned to Peggy during the week and told her he wanted to go to church with us too. They both showed up and I presented Peggy with her first Bible before we went in. She told me she was nervous and when I asked her why she said she had never gone to church before. In fact, she had never been inside a church in her life. Can you imagine the culture shock? She must have been thinking, "What is going on here?" Still, it was a start for them to get on track.

They kept coming to church for a couple months and even started bringing their kids from previous marriages. Then they tried finding a church a little closer to home. I continued to feed Peggy and Don through e-mails to help keep their spirits alive and thriving.

We lost touch for a long time, but one day I got an email from Peggy, about six years later. She said she and Don were married and they and the kids were still going to church. She told me the seed planted that day at Starbucks took deep root and she just wanted to let me know and encourage me to keep serving the Lord. How sweet the sound!

9
Sharing the Faith

"In the beginning..." Those were the first words I remember reading from the Bible back in June 1998, right after I came to know Jesus as my personal Lord and Savior. I soon wanted to lead others to a personal relationship with Him, too. In the beginning, I prayed for success in leading just one person to the Lord. Jesus's sheep know His voice and He will speak the "Word of Truth" through us, to those whose hearts He has prepared. We only need to ask to be used and to pray for guidance and direction. Then we simply step out in faith when the Lord opens the door by bringing us opportunities.

The next four years went quickly. I had a little more experience by then and had shared lots of stories of decisions for Christ with numerous Christians. Many have asked me questions about it. How do you do it? What do you say? How do you get the conversation started? Others would simply say, "I wish I could do that!"

I realized how my stories encourage and energize other believers. We all have a story to tell about our lives, both before and after knowing Jesus. I decided to keep a journal of my experiences. But before long, the task became too daunting because I couldn't keep up with it! Wherever I went, there seemed to be a story of God's divine intervention. Whenever we do something with pleasing the Lord in mind, He just seems to show up and soften the hearts and minds we are there to win over. We are just the messengers. God guides us and arranges the "divine appointments" and we humbly and faithfully deliver the message.

What I have written in this book is a compilation of thoughts, words, and deeds. I have tried to write it as accurately as possible, not to boast, except to boast in the Lord. He points and we simply go. Sharing our faith with the lost is the most challenging, enduring, and exciting thing we can ever do.

We all have a story to tell! If you have hope in your heart, always be ready to give a reason for your hope (1 Peter 3:15, NIV).

All we must do is open our mouths and say something good, something positive, maybe something to provide hope to someone. Remember to smile, encourage, and compliment. Never withhold a spiritual message or thought out of shame or embarrassment! The Scriptures say, "For whoever is ashamed of Me and My words in this adulterous and sinful generation, of him the Son of Man [Jesus] also will be ashamed when He comes in the glory of his Father with the holy angels" (Mark 8:38, NKJV).

I had to face those thoughts early on and the above scripture was seared into my conscience. I found the best way to deal with this situation is to ask the Holy Spirit, "Lord, is this a divine appointment?" We cannot serve out of guilt or obligation because "The Lord loves a cheerful giver" (2 Corinthians 9:7, NASB).

I was excited about Jesus and was reading the Bible continually, praying, and riding to church on my Harley. I rode it everywhere! I had become consumed with Jesus and my bike had become a tool in my war chest. I had no idea what I was in for! I had prayed for a challenging ministry, something I could sink my teeth into, something that would get my adrenaline pumping. Well, I got it! "My cup runneth over" (Psalm 23:5, KJV).

I found I was starving for fellowship with other bikers and, as mentioned earlier, I had joined a local HOG chapter. I soon began to learn about the secular side of things. I began learning from the "lighter weight" bikers on my way up to the hard-core bikers. I had also participated in a Christian riding group at my church. We rode together and had fun, but the club was mostly about recreation and fellowship. I only lasted a couple of weeks because I realized I needed something much deeper, not just for the fun, but for the "calling." I wanted to witness to the lost in an exciting and more challenging way. I didn't know what I didn't know at the time. Throughout the process, I found I needed, like the Apostle Paul, to "... become all things to all men, that I might by all means save some" (1 Corinthians 9:22, NKJV).

10
Finding our Place on the Battlefield

After lots of prayers and witnessing along the way, I had the idea to search the internet to see if there was any such thing as an organized motorcycle ministry. I was still praying for something I could get seriously committed to. It was then that I found there are scores of motorcycle ministries out there. During my search, I found and read up on the Christian Motorcyclists Association or CMA. I contacted them and went through their training. They had sub-ministries within the association, and I chose their Prison Ministry and made a commitment of one year to see if it was right for me.

After the application and testing process, they sent me a CMA back patch and front patches to sew on my Levi cut-off jacket. It was traditional for bikers to wear Levi jackets made into vests by cutting off the sleeves. There were also tons of retailers selling leather biker vests, which are the most popular today. In the biker club vernacular, riding vests are called *cuts*.

I took to the highways and byways, wearing my Christian biker cut and thinking the whole thing seemed pretty cool. The CMA seemed to be an open organization and there was little or no accountability. You could ride a motorcycle of any make or model. Members would create chapters in their respective areas or just run "lone wolf" and unattached. Nobody seemed to care. Also, women could be members and wear the CMA back patch.

I learned a lot about how to share the Word of God without being offensive or obnoxious to the secular bikers and clubs. One weekend I went on a Bill Glass Prison Ministry run with my good friend and Brother in Christ, "Sandman." The large event was called the Weekend of Champions. More than 600 of us from all over California rode our bikes, mostly Harleys, into all the detention facilities in Fresno and the central California area, sharing the Gospel with the inmates.

We were assigned to Corcoran State Prison and rode our motorcycles fifty miles in the rain from Fresno and back for two days. Sandman and I were sent to a level-four maximum security yard with many inmates doing life without parole. Entertainment was provided by celebrities who gave their testimonies at the end of their performances. They then told the inmates to talk to us about Jesus and salvation if they were interested in knowing where they were going when they die, and how to improve the quality of their lives until then.

Including all the jails, juvie halls, prisons, boot camps, and so on, we were told there were around 11,000 inmates in all. I had the incredible privilege and honor of sharing the Gospel with some of them. Spiritual seeds were planted and watered, and many souls were harvested through the power and grace of God. I saw one of our teammates praying with ten inmates at one time while standing in a big circle holding hands!

The forecast was for torrential rain. We would ride sometimes fifty miles in a downpour, and when we got to the prison, the sky would open up and the sun would shine on us through a hole in the blackest clouds I'd ever seen. We rode our Harleys right into the maximum-security prison yard and did laps for the inmates! They

Finding our Place on the Battlefield

went crazy and were cheering us on and giving us the thumbs-up sign. When we would go inside for a break, it would rain, but each time we would resume the sun would break through again. This went on for two days! One of the staff lieutenants said if he ever had any doubts about divine intervention, they were gone forever!

During one break, it started raining again and some of us bikers sought refuge in a prison bus. The biker next to me knelt beside a correctional officer in that wet, crowded bus and led him to the Lord right there. The weekend was an incredible testimony to both prison staff and inmates alike. They had to be impressed how so many sacrificed their safety and comfort and even risked their lives to bring the good news of Jesus to them.

One Arian Brotherhood gang member in for murder told me "Naw man, I ain't ready." The Holy Spirit provided the words he needed to hear, and he gave his heart to Jesus about fifteen minutes later. He hugged me, called me "brother," and told me he loved me. Can you imagine? He then asked me to pray with him for his stepson. He found me at the end of the last day and hugged me and thanked me again. I was told I would never forget what happens at these events and it's true, I never will. Multiply my experiences at Corcoran times 600 teammates and imagine the power of God that was shown! The only word for it is *awesome*!

After putting in a year with CMA, I had learned the basics of motorcycle ministry but still longed for something more challenging. Turns out it was right under my nose, only ten miles north of me.

11

Hardcore

In the acknowledgments at the end of the book, I mention a great friend and brother in the Lord, Robert Garcia, aka "Chapo" (may he rest in peace), who took me under his wing along with Jimmy Moss and brother Joe Cole who we called "Road Dog" (RIP, Joe). They were part of a local chapter of a hardcore motorcycle ministry (which I will leave unnamed) only ten miles up the road from me. Their mother chapter was down in southern California. Most of the members were ex-convicts with some gnarly rap sheets, including murder, attempted murder, armed robbery, grand theft auto, heroin and meth sales, and interstate transportation of illegal drugs for sale. Many had formerly struggled with addictions as well. There was no association more unlikely for me to be involved with than them. After all, I had never been arrested or had any run-ins with the law, ever.

Nonetheless, I was drawn to them. They were all born-again Christians now. They had paid their debt to society, were clean and sober, and didn't indulge in crude jokes or cursing. I had prayed for something outside the box and hardcore, right? Well, there it was, and it was just the beginning.

I had met them at a church barbecue and fundraiser in Santa Maria, forty-five miles to the south, and was approached by them. They impressed me immediately with their appearance and confident demeanor. I knew they were the real deal! Chapo had spotted me first and was compelled to approach me. Wherever Chapo went, his crew was always right there with him. They had all the earmarks of grit but tempered with an aura of peace. It would be hard to explain to a non-believer. I stayed with them at the function and got to know them a little. Afterwards, I was invited to attend a few local runs with them back home. I agreed.

We all got along like family and after about a month Chapo invited me to go through what is called a "hang around" stage with their chapter, and again I accepted. This made me a formal associate. He said it would take some time for me to earn my way in. I told him I would make a one-year commitment and at the end we could both decide if I was a good fit for them.

When I had put in a "respectable" amount of time, I was promoted to "Prospect" (meaning prospective member), which is a non-member position everyone goes through until they are thoroughly vetted, evaluated, and trained on all the dos and don'ts.

Many secular clubs require from six months up to several years or more to prove yourself during the prospect stage. Within the year I was voted on by the chapter members for full membership, which the subculture calls "patched" or "full patch." Each prospective member is always required to receive a 100% approval vote from all the patched members in the chapter they are hoping to join. I got the vote and shortly thereafter was voted in as the new chapter president or "P." This was an unusually quick promotion. I really think I got it because no one else wanted it. I told the guys there was no way I was ready for it, but they insisted and said they would help me to get established.

We wore a two-piece back patch and the "colors" of the Ministry were Black and White. I served the chapter for three-plus years while retaining the rank of president. I was learning the subculture at a very rapid rate because I had to. I was on the fringe of ministering in the real hardcore biker world where mistakes can be costly, as in bodily injury or even death in the worst cases, or an embarrassing "mud check" at best. Mud checks (or gut checks) are verbal, up close, and personal. They meant to put you in your place or to test your mettle. It can be very stressful.

To learn as much as possible as quickly as possible, I found a site on the internet called rcvsmc.org, which stands for Riding Club Versus Motorcycle Club. It was a website filled with different levels of protocol, jargon, and sub-cultural differences. It is still active today as I write this as a place to learn basic to advanced MC protocol. Every pearl of wisdom found there is like a gold nugget that can help you to earn respect and acceptability, as well as keep you safe.

We used to ride from the central California coast, down to the LA area almost monthly for mother chapter gatherings. It was a time of fun, fellowship, and breaking bread. Those events were always followed or preceded by a great church service.

On one of those occasions, there were only two of us from the central coast, Sandman and me. We had stopped at a Mexican fast-food place and were hit up by a guy asking for money. I told him I wouldn't give him money but would buy him a meal. He accepted. Having studied my back patch while we were in line, he asked me if I believed everything in the Bible and I told him yes. He then said, "What about Noah's Ark? Do you believe that too?"

I answered in the affirmative again. I told him, "After all I have studied, it came down to a choice, and I chose to believe it all." I then said, "If there are any untruths found in the Bible, then I wouldn't know what else in the Bible wasn't true and therefore couldn't trust *any* of its content." It took him a while to digest this idea as he worked through his meal. I then shared the message of salvation with him.

He responded, "Man, this is unreal. I just got out of county jail and everyone I run into keeps telling me about Jesus. That's crazy, man!"

I laughed and told him, "Maybe the Lord is calling your name!"

He thoughtfully said, "Maybe. Huh!"

Because we were running late, I gave him a tract with the sinner's prayer and said goodbye. As we started up our Harleys, I looked back over my shoulder at the guy. He waved and shouted, "God Bless!"

We were late and needed to get going, but then I thought for a second and shut my bike down. I got off and walked back to the guy and told him this: "Brother, you know who I am and what I do. You've never seen me before and probably never will again. I've just given you an answer to your troubles. Do you want to ask Jesus into your heart right here and now and have your sins forgiven and be assured of where you will go if you were to die before the sun comes up tomorrow?"

He looked me straight in the eye and said, "Yes." I had almost missed a divine appointment because I was in a hurry to get to church, when in fact I might be the only church this poor soul might ever see! We prayed out loud together holding hands in the traditional biker handshake. A peace seemed to come over him. We hugged and said goodbye again, and as I got back on my bike he again yelled "God bless you" as we roared out of the parking lot.

When I think of warfare in the spiritual realm, I can't help but wonder how many spirits were trying to pull that guy down and how many angels had been sent to lift him up so he could receive Jesus. It was the power of good versus evil. The Lord our God "wishes that none should perish" (2 Peter 3:9, NASB).

12

Enter the Last Disciples MC

In several areas of this book, I refer to outlaw motorcycle clubs by their actual patch or logo colors. "Colors" is a term used to identify the myriad motorcycle clubs out there on the streets and highways. It refers to the primary color or colors of the patches worn on the front and back of their club vest or *cut*. The term has carried over to the denim and leather biker vests worn today.

According to outlaw biker protocol, it can be considered disrespectful to speak or write the name of a club if you are not affiliated with it. Therefore, many use the club colors or designated numbers, instead of actual names. For example, one large dominant club is referred to as HA. Their colors are Red and White (R&W) and their affiliated club number is 81. Since their name abbreviation is HA, the 81 stands for the eighth and first letters of the alphabet. Also, the names of the various club colors are capitalized because they are being used instead of the actual club name. That's how it works so you will better understand as you continue reading.

After more than three years with Chapo and the brothers, we began hearing some concerning reports about the mother chapter down south. There were men's as well as women's rehab homes attached to the ministry down there and we were hearing reports of alleged misconduct. We had also been told there was some drinking and drug use going on, as well as a few other things. It was just hearsay at that point, but when I made a phone call to discuss our concerns I was basically blown off. It just didn't feel right.

So, we called a special meeting of all our Mid-Cal members to discuss the matter in more detail. In the end, all but one member voted to disassociate and shut down our chapter. We wanted a fresh start. I sent the mother chapter a respectful letter of intent to separate from them, along with twenty-three patches from our area.

Afterward, our brothers didn't know whether to scatter or hang together. I stressed how we should stay together and continue meeting and praying for God's direction. The enemy was trying to divide and conquer us. If we split up, Satan would win. I couldn't stand the thought. I felt we needed to form a new club, from the ground up. In the end, only nine members stuck it out through the process.

We started kicking around all sorts of ideas about how hardcore we wanted to go, what colors to choose, what our patch design would look like, and what name we would adopt. It took about six months to make all the decisions and formulate the new bylaws. Looking back, it had been a long, long haul, and one of the greatest challenges of my life.

As we sat around one day at member Pat Kelley's house, we were trying to pick a name for our new club (our "club" was to be our ministry). I blurted out, "Well, we're for sure not the First Disciples." Then Brother Chapo said, "How about the Last Disciples?" The room went silent. We immediately knew it was the name we were looking for. We took a quick vote, and the rest is history. We all agreed to stick with Black and White patch colors because that's what we had worn previously and were comfortable with. All our clothing was in those colors too, so it was a relatively easy choice.

The patch design we settled on was created and gifted to us by Ron Wheeler, a pastor out of SoCal. We were so grateful for his gift we blessed him back with $400 for the design and his support. We found a patch maker in North Hollywood to do a run of new patches for us. I spent $2,600 out of pocket to get us set up, for which the club later voted to reimburse me. We didn't take the design of our new patch lightly. It was White on Black. It was comprised of four pieces for the back, including our club name, center logo, slogan, and a diamond with the letters MC.

We had other patches and tags made up for the front as well, including a front diamond with our logo and the number 777 representing the Father, the Son, and the Holy Spirit. Each patch we wear has a biblical significance, and all patches are proprietary and are worn by Last Disciples members only. When someone asks about the meaning of a patch, as they so frequently do, they have just in effect opened the Bible to receive a spiritual answer. The public seems to love the exchange. The outlaws liked it too. Deep down, everyone is searching. They just don't want to be beaten over the head with the Bible in the process. It must be done gently and with reverence.

Below is an explanation of who we are today and what we do. More can be found on our website at LastDisciples.com.

The Last Disciples MC is a registered 501(c)(3) non-profit organization. As such, we are a soul-winning Christian motorcycle club that reaches out to bikers, gang members, street people, at-risk youths, those with any life-controlling addiction, and those who have "fallen through the cracks" of conventional ministry. We purpose to maintain a strong ministry of evangelism, discipleship, education, brotherhood, and prayer for the purpose of meeting needs, healing hurts, and reconciling souls back to God.

Our club colors are Black and White. They represent our belief that God's message of salvation does not have any gray areas. Our top rocker, Last Disciples, means "When all others turn from the

Lord, we shall remain faithful, even unto being the Last Disciples!" When queried, I often tell folks, "I may very well be 'the last disciple' to share the message of salvation with you before you are called to judgment." It's a sobering thought but has always been well received.

Our center patch represents a place called Golgotha, which in Hebrew means "the place of a skull" and it's where Jesus was crucified. On the third day, He rose from the dead and was seen, conversed with, and touched by over 500 witnesses. His resurrection defeated death. It gives new meaning to the words "No fear!"

Jesus put a smile on the face of Death for all who believe in Him. We can now laugh in Satan's face, for we know with certainty where we are going when we die. Death is just the beginning of our new spiritual journey.

We have been criticized by a few for wearing a skull on our backs as a Christian motorcycle club, but to us, it's not demonic, nor an icon to be worshipped, but instead has a very special meaning to us. Our bottom rocker quotes our motto, from Revelation 2:10 "... faithful unto death..." (KJV). The MC means we are a motorcycle club. We accept Christian men only and the criteria are strict.

We come from a variety of backgrounds and have experienced the hard knocks and realities of life and death in the real world. We no longer live just for ourselves. We are now hardcore for Jesus! We are also a neutral club. As such, we offer help to anyone and everyone who needs it. We are non-territorial and do not engage in any type of criminal or gang-related activity. We endeavor to be a threat to none and a friend to all.

Our club is our ministry, a brotherhood, a way of life, serving the Lord through loving and serving one another, our communities, and those in need of help. We are promised in the Bible that those of us who believe and trust in Jesus for our salvation will be saved from eternal darkness, eternal torment, and eternal separation from

God. We want to share this confidence and assurance with others. The message of salvation is so simple even a small child can understand it. We are the messengers.

13

Divine Intervention

Now that you know who we are and how we got here, this is where things go from informative to dicey. In the world of biker clubs, you can't just make up a patch and go. One must follow long-established protocols. This is a subculture and those who are on the outside are unaware. There is a pecking order. The first order of business when starting a new club (whether Christian or not) is to contact the local "dominant" MC. This would be the largest and most powerful club running in your riding area or planned area of operations. You must contact them and arrange a sit-down meeting.

At the time of the sit-down (if granted) you will respectfully layout your intentions. You see, the dominant clubs police the other clubs within their area, from the biggest down to the smallest. If you don't follow the protocol, you will be setting up yourself, and other members-in-waiting, for a bad experience. Maybe a beat-down, run off the road, stabbed, or even shot. This is very serious business to the real deal biker clubs. Some of whom may be involved in illegal activities. Whether that's the case or not, they need to know who you are and what you're about, like if you allow cops in your club, or if you're affiliated with one or more of their enemies. This is how the subculture operates.

The dominant club in every state and county will usually be a 1% club or sometimes a shared hierarchy of 1% clubs. The 1% clubs are the rebel bikers who rule by fear, force, and respect, and who flip the bird at the law, while the other 99% of motorcycle clubs are made up of law-abiding citizens (an old decree by the American Motorcyclist Association). The 1%ers usually choose to keep to themselves and their supporters unless protocol enforcement is needed. Then they "TCB," meaning take care of business!

The MC world is a very serious undertaking (no pun intended). It is as serious to them as it gets. Some of them may be friendly and others may be deadly serious and easily offended. You must understand this before we get deeper into it. The basic rule is to assume nothing! If a person wants to get into one of the big secular clubs, you don't ask about membership. If they are interested in you, they may approach you based on who knows you, your street reputation, and how you handle yourself. If you seem like a good fit, they may invite you to show up at a few functions. After a while, if all goes well, you may be asked to be a "hang around."

The process goes from a Hang Around to being made a Prospect, and then a Full Patch member. It can easily take a year or two to work into a 1% club. In the secular world, the club comes before all things, including family and job. If at some point they get converted to faith, they then have a big struggle between choosing worldly things and truly walking with the Lord. It becomes a conundrum for them.

The top guns of the biker world are the 1%er clubs who usually wear a diamond shaped patch on the front and/or the back of their cuts. It may also have a "1%" or "1%er" symbol inside the diamond. The complete "back patch" will often consist of three, four, or even five separate pieces but is commonly referred to as a three-piece patch. There are lots of them scattered around, but there are only about a dozen powerful, well-known 1%er MCs in the US. Below them in status are the three-piece MCs who do not wear the diamond. They are also hardcore but not nearly as powerful as the

1%ers. Many of them are support clubs or affiliates of the dominant clubs in their respective areas.

Below the three-piece clubs are the two-piece and one-piece clubs (with a few exceptions) that are most often lightweight smaller social riding clubs or associations. Separate from the above are specialized MCs comprised of all Christian members, which may or may not be held to higher standards. Some call themselves a CMC (Christian motorcycle club) and wear mostly two or three-piece patches. They too will be held accountable by the dominant clubs in their areas. Christian or not, you will still be expected to conform to basic protocol if you are wearing a club-type back patch. There are also biker clubs out there specializing in drug and alcohol rehab issues. Likewise, there are even clubs for firefighters, law enforcement, and military vets too. If you can think of it, it probably exists.

As you can see, it is all quite complex. If you are going into the arena as a Christian MC, you had better know your stuff. You can be sure the lessons never end, and the learning never stops. Some 1%er clubs are autonomous, allowing their chapters to call their own shots (within their national guidelines). Others are more strictly guided by their national chapter, sometimes referred to as the "mother chapter," and protocol can vary from region to region, state to state, and club to club. What is unimportant to one club may be a big deal to another. All you can do is know your turf and everyone interacting within it. *Respect* is paramount. You will usually get what you give. It's always best to stay in your lane and not get cocky.

Once up and running, the Last Disciples established an affiliate ministry called Black Ops International. It was created for places where back patches can't be worn due to either the laws of the land or in cases where the dominants have not yet been contacted. The cuts have identifying patches on the front, but no patches are worn on the back. For some men, regardless of location, it's a good fit because it allows them to minister without having to deal with MC politics. In some countries such as Australia, there are certain states or areas where established motorcycle clubs are no longer allowed to fly their colors (club back patches). Our faithful Aussie reps such as "Stev" for Last Disciples MC and Eagle Eye Mike for Black Ops International have done an incredible job paving the way for us in their respective territories.

Needless to say, in today's world a group of guys wanting to start a new Christian MC with a three-piece patch and diamonds is very difficult. Sure, there are also some softcore, one-piece and two-piece patch faith-based clubs, but they pretty much stay away from the hardcore nasty challenges. Don't get me wrong, I'm not knocking anyone here, they all have their purpose and mission. But just for clarification, the most hardcore of the faith-based clubs are the ones wearing the three-piece back patches.

The Last Disciples voted to go as deep as we could go. Our philosophy was, if you can minister to the absolute toughest of the secular clubs, then everyone else along the way should be a cakewalk. Made sense to me. Also, among the serious clubs, whether Christian or secular, almost all have a Harley-only rule. The reason is, if you ride a Harley, you will have a greater chance of being accepted by *everyone* out there. After all, everyone appreciates and respects the Harley brand. Not so with a Honda Goldwing or a Japanese crotch rocket. Everything must be thought out, played out, and prayed out to the max!

The established clubs, even the Christian ones, often resist new clubs starting up in their areas. It can be confusing and worrisome to them, which is why the dominant club controls everything in their area. Are you a friend or a foe? They want to know who's who and who gave you a "green light" to fly your club colors. Even the established and approved Christian clubs tend to resist other Christians from coming into their areas or turf. I know this may sound dumb but it's all about control. The Christian clubs are often concerned about weak or phony "Christian" clubs coming into their areas of operation with false doctrine, adding to the confusion of those they have been ministering to. The Bible warns about many coming in the name of Jesus who will preach false doctrine. As you can see, the mission is very challenging.

One time we had one of our motorcycles vandalized by a well-known motorcycle "ministry." The rear tire had been flattened, and the President of that club left his business card on the seat of the bike saying, "I wish I could have given this to you in person!" We had already been cleared by the dominant MC, but the Christian club didn't want us around. They even followed up with a threat of physical harm if we were to try expanding into their area of southern California. They already knew us well. It was just internal politics and fear tactics. It wasn't long before we had a crew established there. Sometimes you've got to know when to flex and not be pushed around by a non-dominant club. Fortunately, there were no more issues after that.

Starting a new MC like the Last Disciples attracts a lot of attention. Once the word gets out it spreads quickly. After all, the secular clubs (especially the dominants) don't need the extra headaches of newcomers in town. What's in it for them? They don't "get" how true Christians have something they need. So why should they let a new Christian club in? Protocol and the rules of respect dictate you announce who you are and what you are planning to do. But they may simply tell you to pound sand. You must be prepared to answer some very tough questions! And your answers must be true, compelling, and delivered with confidence, a steady hand, and unwavering eye contact.

How did the Last Disciples get a foot in the door to even have hope of a sit-down with our dominant? Well, it started with three of our co-founders, all former members of our old club. Not one of us had any connections within the dominant club in our area of California. We had heard the R&W claimed our county but neither they nor any other 1% club had members living here at the time.

There was, however, a smaller MC in the middle of our area with about fifty years of running in San Luis Obispo County and other parts of California. Their colors are Black and Gold. We had known and supported them on their runs and fundraisers for about four years when we were with our former club. We contacted their founder and national president and asked him if they would have any problem with us dropping our old patch and starting a new club with a new patch and running the same members. He graciously gave us a thumbs up because we were using the same guys he already knew and was comfortable with. But we still needed and hoped for more juice from the nearest 1% club, which brought us back to needing a sit-down with the R&W.

To the non-biker, overhearing a conversation between club members can sometimes sound coded, and at times it is, with clubs being referred to by their colors or numbers. There is a common nomenclature one learns when living the lifestyle. For Last Disciples, "L" is the twelfth letter of the alphabet and "D" is the fourth, so our number is 124.

Because our colors were Black and White, there could be a conflict with our dominant (Red and White) because one of their long-time enemies also wears black and white colors. However, that club's colors I'm talking about here are black graphics on a white background while ours are white graphics on a black background. Maybe, just maybe, our colors would be accepted and we would be "blessed" in by 81, not to mention any other club(s) who may fly black and white colors too. I should note how none of the clubs, big or small, have any obligation to accept a new club, especially when it appears there's nothing in it for them.

At this point, I think it's appropriate to mention how some of the clubs identifying themselves as Christian are nothing more than phony, judgmental hypocrites. They earn those titles through un-Christian-like behavior, such as public drunkenness, gawking at the wet T-shirt contests, and using rude and abusive language. They might better be described as "secular Christians." Due to poor behavior by some, the secular clubs may automatically think you're just dirtbags hiding behind a Cross hoping to fit in or get preferential treatment. It is our fervent hope to show them a difference and to reverse the damage done by those still walking in darkness instead of the Light.

In addition to the R&W, we also needed to acquire a thumbs-up from another super-dominant in our state, known as the Black and White Nation who, like R&W, are scattered not only around the state of California but are nationwide and international as well. In addition to this, we would also need a sit-down with the "Greens" as well as the Blue and White. All are massive and powerful organizations. And this was just the beginning. It seemed like a person would be more likely to win the lottery than for us to pull off something like this. No doubt it was a huge challenge, except for our ace in the hole: Jesus! "I can do all things through Christ who strengthens me" (Philippians 4:13, NKJV).

So, what do you do to overcome those who would not understand our true mission and make uncool comments about our purpose and credibility? You pray! "God, if this is your will, please light up our path and soften the hearts of those who would come against us. In Jesus's name we pray. Amen." That was our prayer and the direction we hoped for. One of our charter members, "Duppy"

Munoz, knew someone who knew someone (one of those deals). He simply made a cold call through personal channels and then we hoped for the best.

14
RED & WHITE, VENTURA

ONE EVENING, ONLY a week or so later, I got a call from the Ventura president of the R&W. It was the man himself, a long-time president of his chapter. What? Was I hearing the caller correctly? Was this for real or just *surreal*? We must have talked for a half-hour. Before we finished, he asked me if we could come down to Ventura to meet him. I was still in shock a man of his stature in the biker world would even give me the time of day! He even went on to say he would come to me if he could, but he had just had hip surgery and it would be easier for him if we would come down south.

At this point, you might ask yourself if you believe in miracles, or just in coincidences. As you continue to read on, there will be coincidences that the odds, common sense, and logic would never support. Yes, I have seen and believe in miracles. And the more I see, the more I pray, and the more I pray, the more I see. It's been nothing short of mind-blowing. But that's just me. As Bill O'Reilly (formerly with FOX News) used to say, "I'm just a simple man."

As I traded stories with this guy, he made me feel comfortable. He was a complete gentleman and easy to talk with. As our conversation continued about our hopeful club, he said he had been wanting to find "a support club" up in our area. I was obliged to tell him straight up we could not be an exclusive supporter for anyone, except Jesus. His next comment took me by surprise. He said, "That's fine, I'd still like to meet you in person so we can see what you guys are all about." I was thinking it could have been some built-in paranoia to determine if we were maybe infiltrators trying to work our way in to gather inside intelligence or something. After all, this wasn't his first rodeo as he had been in the game for more than forty years!

Before we hung up, he mentioned the weather report was looking like rain. "If it's raining just drive, you don't need to impress me," he said with a hint of humor.

I replied, "Heck Pres, we ride rain or shine, that's what it's all about."

"There it is," he said in return with a laugh. We had a pleasant conversation, discussing relationships and the ups and downs of marriage, and other lighter topics as well.

We set a date for the sit-down and I began thinking about who I should take with me. I chose fellow cofounders Pat Kelley and brother Chapo. The day we left for Ventura was damp as I recall but not raining. Chapo and I rode while Pat ran "chase" for us in his truck since his Harley was down. We got there after dark and had planned to be there early to show respect. It was also a sign of respect to take only a modest number of guys to a sit-down unless told otherwise. One never knows the number of dominant club members who will be present. And it is never good to outnumber your sit-down hosts unless of course you're in the mood to get tossed out on your ear. That would be embarrassing, especially since we're not only supposed to be representing our club, but were also called to be ambassadors for Christ.

Upon arrival at the R&W clubhouse, we immediately noticed it was on a darkish backstreet. Their compound was surrounded by chain-link fencing. There were prospective members scattered about for security. As soon as we rolled in, the prospects directed us where to park. We were then escorted into the clubhouse. Inside the front door was the main trophy room. The walls and bookshelves were heavy with impressive memorabilia. There were plaques, trophies, and lots of pictures. Closed-circuit cameras and screens were in place and made a serious impression.

As we were being escorted in, the infamous R&W president arrived with his entourage in a large, shiny black SUV, such as you might see in a presidential motorcade. They were escorted by a crew of R&W on gleaming, deafening Harleys.

After we were led inside by some prospects, the president and the chapter officers walked in a few moments later. He looked at me and said, "Are you Lou?" I said I was, and as we shook hands he said, "I thought you'd look different." I didn't know if this was good or bad. I guess I should have been nervous, but I was excited and felt confident. Our new crew, their families, and our churches were all praying for us. We felt we had done everything we could to prepare for what was to come. I had even told our guys if God was for us then nothing could stop us.

But, if we got it all wrong and God was *not* backing us, then we might just die as martyrs for a noble cause (at least in *our* minds). What better way to die? After all, we were simply trying to serve the Kingdom of God. Then I thought if we only got a beat-down and were thrown out, we would know for sure God didn't have our backs on this crazy endeavor. If that were the case, then we would have to rethink everything and find another way to serve God, maybe giving away free snow cones and Bible tracts at the beach while singing Amazing Grace in harmony, a cappella (Lord forbid). It has been said the Lord has endless ways of humbling us.

The president led us into the bar area of the clubhouse where there was a semi-circle of high barstools set up facing a low leather couch. We were told to sit on the couch, which felt way too low. The room was silent as the R&W officers took their seats on the barstools, looking down upon us. One of them was their sergeant-at-arms. He appeared to be about a 350-pounder. He was a massive man. His presence was so impressive I can hardly remember what the others looked like!

Then the president asked me to introduce my brothers. With the formalities taken care of, he pretty much wanted me to tell his crew who we were and what we wanted. This was the easy part. Then he started a question-and-answer session. It was a little tense but that's the way it's supposed to work. We were locked down, on their property, and it was now time to find out what we were made of.

After I provided some general information, the president got down to the nitty-gritty. Looking me straight in the eye he said, "I got a question for you. Jesus was a Christian, right? And one of His right-hand men was a guy named Judas, right?" I nodded and replied in the affirmative. "Well, that guy ratted out Jesus, didn't he? So, if Jesus couldn't trust one of His closest guys, why should we trust you?"

It might have been a tough question for some people, but I was well versed in the Scriptures, having read a variety of Bibles cover to cover, so I had an answer for him. I told him I only knew what the Bible had to say about the topic. I told him, "The Bible says Satan entered into Judas," gazing at each member looking down on us in characteristic interrogation style. I continued, "Just like he could enter into you and you and you and you and you, and me as well. Judas had an evil plan he had worked out to get thirty pieces of silver as his bribe if he would show the Roman cohort where and who Jesus was and snitch Him off. He was greedy and had been deceived by Satan. Judas had been thinking in the 'here and now' about things many men lust over."

I then told them how after Judas was paid the blood money, he was so distraught about what he had done he threw the money back into a temple and then went out and hung himself.

The president said, "Wow, I always wondered about that!" What could have been a "got ya" question turned out to be a perfect one.

At one point during the interview, the huge sergeant was making a statement about his opinion on something I had said, and I instinctively began shaking my head in the negative. He then raised his voice and boomed at me, "Don't shake your [expletive] head when I'm talking to you. You don't have a clue what I'm about to say."

I smiled at him, nodded, and made a hand gesture for him to continue his comment. What he was saying had been incorrect, so after he had finished speaking, I looked at the president and asked, "Sir, may I respond to what the gentleman said?" He nodded his assent. I then addressed the sergeant and cleared the air, not skipping a beat. I assured him we were there to serve the biker community, to provide spiritual counsel, to marry and bury, and share our knowledge of the Bible with any of their members who may want or need to talk about spiritual matters.

Then the sergeant boomed again, pointing a huge finger at me, "You won't find any of our guys who want to hear anything you have to say!" In response, I smiled again at the sergeant and stared at him for several seconds. Then he got a smile on his face, broke eye contact, and looking up at the ceiling he said, "Well, maybe a few." The room then erupted into laughter and the ice was broken. I then told him I was there even if for only one.

It was very cool seeing the Holy Spirit clearing the way. Only a real Christian believer could understand the feeling. It was as if the Holy Spirit (who indwells believers) was speaking for and through me. It felt smooth and easy. As a Christian man, I am unwilling to lie and will avoid it at all costs (so help me Lord). I knew we had to be everything the R&W might be expecting from men who call themselves Christians. Our honesty was then tested by the president's next question. "Let me ask you this," he said. "If one of our enemies came to you asking for help, would you help them?"

I didn't hesitate. "Yes, I would. We wouldn't help them *against* you, but we would support their spiritual needs just like we would for your club or anyone else. We serve God but stay out of the club politics while doing so."

The president glanced at his guys, then at me, and said he appreciated my candid answer. I then told him I'd never lie to him, to which he said to me, "And we will never lie to you either."

As we continued, the aura in the room became relaxed and friendly as the president asked all his guys their opinion on allowing us to fly our patches on their turf. One by one each member stated if the rest of our guys were like us, they thought it would be a good thing. "But don't change," they added. Then the president said he would expect us to support their fundraisers and rallies. I assured him that's exactly what we wanted to do, adding that if the other clubs invited us to their functions, we would be obliged to do the same for them as well.

Next, he asked if they would see us in any of the bars as we attended functions. I told him we go into bars all the time. "That's what Jesus would have done. We don't drink or smoke, but we don't judge those who do either."

Then he said, "If you see me in a bar are you gonna buy me a drink?"

I replied, "Well, maybe. It depends on whether you're nice to me or not." Again, everyone broke into laughter.

Then he said, "Well, it's time to open the bar, so you guys may want to cut out. I think we're finished here."

As we started to go, they gave us hugs and handshakes and wished us well. Then Chapo brought something up I had forgotten about in all the excitement. As we started to go, he whispered, "Hey Lou, do you want to show them our patch?" Chapo had them in his hand in a Manilla envelope the whole time we were sitting there.

"Oh, I forgot!" I replied. Chapo then dug into the package and started laying out our patch design on the couch, which must have been designed for short-legged midgets.

The president, who had overheard Chapo, said, "You mean you already had them made?"

"Yes, I did," I replied.

He then looked at his crew and said with a smile, "That's confidence!"

As mentioned earlier, I had already spent $2,600 on our custom Last Disciples MC patches, having found a patch maker in North Hollywood who was known for making patches for some of the big California outlaw clubs. I had felt so sure God had His hand on us that I wanted to have them ready to go as soon as we got our thumbs-up. Otherwise, it would have delayed our moving forward by weeks if not more. We had already faxed our design art to R&W Ventura in advance so they would have time to look it over before the sit-down. Turned out nobody had checked the fax machine and they never saw it.

As Chapo laid out the patches on the black leather couch you could have heard a pin drop. The silence was deafening. The top rocker had "Last Disciples" and the bottom rocker had "Faithful unto Death" (Revelation 2:10, KJV). In the mix was our Diamond MC patch and in the middle of the arrangement was our center patch logo of a smiling skull wearing a helmet with a spike on top. The design practically screamed *outlaw*, which was what we had intended.

The room was silent for a little too long until one of the guys said, "Uhh... that's outlaw!"

"Yes, it is," I replied. "After all, in God's eyes, we're all outlaws. We've broken all or most of His commandments, often daily. We don't think we're better than anyone else, we're just forgiven. That's part of the message we came to share."

Then the president said, "Well, since you're not going to be a support club for us, you'll have to stand up for your own patch. We won't help you if you get called out."

I agreed, saying we come in peace but also have a job to do, and that job is to reach out to the MC culture to lend a hand and an ear to those who are wanting to find peace and answers in their lives.

I went on to tell the silent group staring at our patches how most of our cofounders were ex-cons and we'd be happy to compare rap sheets with any of their members and I bet we'd have them beat. They all smiled and shook their heads saying, "Okay, keep it real!" We all laughed and shook hands again as we were led to the front door.

As we walked out of the compound we didn't speak. It was over. I think we were a little numbed by the fact God had surely gone before us and prepared the hearts who would be judging us. It was like we were shell-shocked but in a positive way. It felt awesome and we were all ecstatic as we pulled into a coffee shop to discuss what had just occurred. The ride home in the cool night air was like riding on clouds. It had been a day we would never forget. It seemed as if we had just experienced a miracle, and in fact, we had! What were the odds?

15

Good to Go!

After getting the green light from R&W, I had my patches sewn on at The Leather Shop in Morro Bay. That day was April 1, 2006. I flew the first Last Disciple MC patch in the wind that day. To add to the joy, my son Ryan, who was now a grown man, called me up and said, "Hey Dad, I bought a Harley." I was elated! On our first ride together, I couldn't stop smiling. There we were, father and son, riding side by side down the freeway, "outlaw style." Ryan was born again by then but not yet drawn to a ministry. We continue riding together to this day.

Soon after getting blessed-in, our club was invited to attend an R&W national rally at Lake Casitas. It was a great event, and we were made welcome. We saw the Ventura president and the big sergeant again and visited for a while.

As we walked around visiting the vendor booths and meeting club members, an amazing thing happened. I introduced myself to a guy who looked familiar. He was wearing Green and White colors with a president tag on the front. His road name was "Ripper." He was also wearing a pin depicting the outline of a fish. So, I asked him if he was a Christian. "Born and raised," he proudly responded. I then asked, "Born again?" as the Bible describes believers and followers of Jesus.

He wasn't quite sure what I meant by my question. As we talked, he became very interested, so I was led to share the message of salvation with him. Within minutes we were praying the sinner's prayer together. Afterward, he was so happy he called a few of his chapter brothers over to meet us.

When I mentioned he looked familiar, he humbly told me he had done a few movies. Believe it or not, the guy I had just prayed with was Robert Patrick, the cyborg "T-1000" cop from *Terminator II: Judgement Day*. I later found out he had also played in *Die Hard 2* and a bunch of other blockbuster movies. It was one of those great moments. He was not only a 1%er president but also a movie star—not something that happens every day!

Sandman, from our old ministry, was not in our new club at the time. He was still flying with the Soldiers for Jesus MC (he later reunited with us and became a Last Disciple). He lived several hours east of me, in Fresno. We had been talking about riding to the next Sturgis rally in September.

When September rolled around, we hooked up and started the 1,450-mile, 22-hour journey north. Of course, it takes longer when you've got to stop for gas about every 150 to 200 miles. But the ride was awesome. The farther north we got the more motorcycles we saw on the road. The Sturgis rally can draw over a half million bikes for the week-long fun fest. This would be my second time there, but my first time in a Last Disciples cut. Sandman was wearing his Soldiers for Jesus Yellow and Black colors.

As it turned out, the Soldiers for Jesus had a booth set up inside a vacant building, along with R&W who were selling apparel. There was also a tattoo booth set up, but the building was mostly occupied by R&W. As we walked through the front door together the room got quiet as all eyes appeared to be on me due to the Black and White colors I was wearing (with diamonds no less). It was one of those moments that kind of hung in the air as we walked through. It was as if no one knew how to respond.

When we got to the Soldier's booth at the back, the feeling was kind of the same. I think everyone was caught a little off guard. At first glance from the front, our cuts look somewhat like those of the 1% Black and White Nation, who have been mortal enemies of the R&W for decades. I made every effort to smile and shake hands with those who made eye contact with me. According to club protocol, which can vary a little, it is proper to introduce yourself with your name, the name of your club, your rank, and where you are from.

While at their booth, a Soldier for Jesus introduced himself as he eyed me cautiously. He then said he would like to pray with me later. I told him, "Absolutely." I immediately knew his intent. He needed to know if I was a "real deal" Christian or a possible infiltrator, maybe trying to get close to the R&W for some nefarious intent. Since Sandman was a member of the Soldiers, and their club was sharing space with the R&W, the guy wanted to make sure nothing would come back on them, should things go bad. Sandman was also approached privately and was asked if I was okay.

We stayed inside but Sandman and I had separated and were talking with others present. After a while the pressure I felt in my spirit became overwhelming and I felt I needed to step outside. When I did, I noticed a sidewalk bench with a group of Christian bikers hanging around it. I walked over and introduced myself to them and was greeted warmly.

I told them I was feeling pressure in my spirit and asked if they would pray for me. At my request, the guys almost stumbled over one another to lay hands on me and pray. It was their purpose for being there and they felt blessed to oblige. I could immediately feel relief. Afterward, I thanked the brothers and went back inside.

When I went in, there was an R&W standing on a ladder nailing something to a wooden beam. I needed to walk by the ladder, near which another R&W was standing. I smiled and said to him, "Do you think it's safe for me to walk past him with that hammer in his hand?"

The guy smiled and said, "You never know," at which we both laughed. I should mention here how the R&W has been rumored to use common hammers as weapons in times of conflict. Some of them who have done so may be seen wearing a pin on the front of their cuts depicting a hammer.

I then grabbed Sandman so we could go out and about and take a little ride. The atmosphere at the Sturgis rally was always intense. There was such a roar from all the bikes it was like standing on the tarmac of a busy international airport. It was a constant, intense adrenaline rush—and I loved it! All the attendees at the rally were happy and friendly. They were in their element.

It did, however, make me think a little about Sodom and Gomorrah. There, riding on the main strip of the little town you might see Grandpa and Granny riding an antique Harley with a sidecar, and right behind them, you might see a topless woman wearing pasties, chaps, and a G-string. It is about as worldly as it gets, from one end of the spectrum to the other. As a Christian, you need to be well prayed up and guard your mind and eyes not to gaze upon the temptations. They were everywhere!

Sandman and I took a ride out to the Full Throttle Saloon for lunch and to do what we do. Later, after sundown, we returned to the Soldiers' booth so Sandman could check in with his club. While there I noticed some activity outside the back door and wandered out. There were lots of bikers and R&W members conversing in the smallish parking area. I noticed a young guy with no legs in a wheelchair drinking a beer. Under his seat was a six-pack of more beer. I started talking with the guy and he told me he was riding drunk one night and when he approached a railway intersection, he tried to speed across to beat a train about to cross. He didn't make it and lost both his legs in the process.

I asked him how he was getting by and if he had gotten past the trauma and was doing okay mentally and spiritually. I told him I was a Christian and my purpose in Sturgis was to help anyone who needed a spiritual boost. He then told me he wanted to trust and follow God but was kind of stuck in a bad place. At this point, the Holy Spirit took over and we had a good talk about God and the Scriptures.

When I asked Him if he wanted to invite Jesus into his heart to strengthen and guide him, he teared up and said, "Yes." I took a knee beside him as he took my hand and prayed the sinner's prayer with me. I could tell his heart was really in it. Afterward, as we said goodbye, he gave me a big hug and thanked me as he reached under his seat and took the six-pack out, throwing it over his head into a dumpster. He smiled and said, "I won't be needing that anymore." I should note how, as this incident happened, we were surrounded by R&W members who were hanging out. As I knelt and prayed with the young guy, I knew with certainty God would have my back. Those are the moments that make all the pain, worries, and dangers worthwhile! I slept well that night, having been blessed with another cookie from Heaven.

The next day, as Sandman and I strolled casually through town, I noticed the booth of a knife vendor. I was drawn to talk with the owner and look at his display. He wasn't busy, so I was able to drop a few seeds about our faith. The guy never hesitated to take it further. He opened his heart to me right then and there and said he needed God in his life and had been feeling it. As I realized the guy was a true divine appointment, I explained the Gospel's message of salvation given to me by the Holy Spirit, just for him. I asked him if he wanted to pray Jesus into his heart and he said yes. Just as soon as we had agreed to pray, potential customers started to crowd in. I told him I didn't want to interfere with his customers and would wait. But he said, "No, they can wait. This is more important!" He then took my hand and prayed with me in front of God and everybody. I traded contact info with him, and Sandman and I went on our way.

When we rode back to California after the event, we gave out lots of tracts along the way. We always do. Since I became saved through the little tract my sister had given me years before, I never wanted to miss an opportunity.

16

Learning the Ropes

Several years had passed since we first hooked up with the R&W in Ventura. We had no idea at the time where our endeavor would lead. Lots had happened since then. We had followed up with sit-downs in Fresno and Sacramento and again were given a green light to fly our patch in those areas. It helped that we had members living in or very near those areas to represent us and to show support at all the biker functions. This kept us in the light and reinforced our credibility. We must always be who we say we are and do what we say we'll do.

Our membership was growing, but so were the challenges. We have a strict application and vetting process as well as a prospecting period. Even so, it's very hard to get to know someone in just one short year of the process, and many of our candidates were not living as close to their sponsors as would be ideal. Sometimes we would do all we could do, pray, and then vote on the person.

As with all MCs, Christian or not, bad apples sometimes slip through the cracks. Then, when the dominant club in their area catches them doing something insulting, disrespectful, or downright unacceptable, something must be done, like immediately. Years of planning and boots-on-the-ground efforts can be lost immediately, sometimes over just one incident! We have now been through the process many times over the years, weeding guys out and pulling their patches. All patches and accessories bearing the Last Disciples name belong to the club and must be returned upon resignation or dismissal, except in instances of service retirement.

After a club is blackballed from an area, it can take years to be forgiven and allowed back in. It often requires a changing of the guard within the dominant chapter before it can happen. Possible reinstatement is never a guarantee. It happened to us several times in the past, due to a member's mistakes. But with us, God has always provided a way. You must learn humility and diplomacy, to be patient, and to wait upon the Lord. We have found that if we do our part right, God will bless our efforts. All pride and vanity must be surrendered to the Lord. And above all else, the glory for the victories must go to God and Him alone.

Pride is one of man's greatest enemies and God hates pride (Proverbs 8:13, NIV). It's a tough walk because pride is what often motivates our flesh to sin. We must continue to seek and praise the Lord in all we do. When we get saved, we become "new creations in Christ" (2 Corinthians 5:17, NASB) and the Holy Spirit indwells us. It becomes our challenge not to "grieve the Holy Spirit" (Ephesians 4:30, NASB).

Once we become sons of God we are no longer "of this world" (John 17:16, NASB). We are only able to overcome our weaknesses through the power of the Holy Spirit. And once we realize this, then "all things are possible through Christ who strengthens me [us]" (Philippians 4:13, KJV). We become believers in the supernatural and the reality of spiritual warfare (see Ephesians 6:12).

There is truly no other explanation for the many things we have seen. Father God is real, Jesus is real, and the Holy Spirit is real. It has taken me twenty-four years to get to where I am today, and I realize now more than ever how the learning process never ends. It continues until we are called Home. The more we ask, the more He reveals. The more we seek, the more we find. And if we repent (turn from our sins and confess them to the Lord), He will forgive us, wipe our slate clean, and incline His ear to our prayers. The power can be enormous! We can get access to this power simply through faith and obedience.

Why are we all here in the first place? The answer is to follow and praise God and to tell the whole world He loves them and how salvation from the pit of Hell lies in His son, Jesus the Christ (which means "the anointed one"). God sent His only begotten Son as the perfect sacrifice (the sacrificial Lamb of God) to die for our sins so all who believe in Him shall not perish but will be saved from eternal damnation.

My walk with God, by way of surrender and submission to Him, has been the most rewarding thing I have ever experienced in my life. I wouldn't change a thing. If anything, I want more! The more I learn, the more I can help others. That's my motivation. It is the best "addiction" we can have! I used to wear a patch back in the early days of my walk with the Lord. It said "A2J" which stood for "Addicted to Jesus." I can't tell you how many conversations that patch started for me!

17

The Red & Gold – Red River Part 1

As word about us got around the internet, I got a call one day from Espanola, New Mexico. It was from a guy who I will call Jose. He said he knew many of the Red and Gold in the Santa Fe area and wanted to discuss starting a Last Disciples chapter there. We took the time it takes to discuss all the protocols and options as well as the application process, vetting, and training. Jose jumped through all the hoops and made an appointment with the local R&G to have a sit-down. Since they already knew who he was, they agreed to meet up at a private rendezvous somewhere in the desert country.

When Jose showed up, there were about ten R&G waiting. If you've never been around their club, I can attest to how they make a formidable impression. They often wear red bandanas to cover their faces in traditional outlaw fashion. Although Jose knew a few of them, the meeting was very serious. They surrounded him and asked what he wanted. After he told them who we (the Last Disciples) are and what we do, they told him they would have to meet our mother chapter officers from "Califa" first. The meeting ended well, but with no guarantees. If it was going to happen, there was a lot of work to be done. For starters, our core leadership was over 1,000 miles away.

Afterward, I got a call bringing me up to date. The New Mexico R&G was about to host their National Annual Run in Red River. It was suggested we show up there if we wanted to continue the talks.

The LDMC Mother Chapter got their act together and left the California coast on our way to the R&G rally in Red River. We had only a four-member crew able to make the 1,000-mile trek. It can be dangerous when crossing club borders while wearing club colors (patches). The politics are forever changing, and our Black and White colors are among the most controversial. However, they bring the outlaw bikers to us in our travels and the rest is in the hands of the Holy Spirit who guides us and speaks through us. In this instance, the R&G had already guaranteed us safe passage as we crossed through New Mexico on our way to the sit-down.

As usual on our trips, we had many divine appointments along the way during food and gas stops. You never know the impact of friendliness, a cheerful voice, sincere encouragement, prayer, and a cool little tract placed in someone's hand.

Our mission was to get blessed into New Mexico. Our representative Jose had set it up for us and we were responding to their invitation for a sit-down with the Santa Fe president and the R&G national president from Texas. Our first order of business, per their instructions, was to show up at the Bull of the Woods Saloon in Red River.

When we arrived on the main strip of the Run, I made a call and our R&G host answered. He told me where to show up and how they would take it from there. As I recall, there were five of us altogether. There was Chapo, Pat Kelly, Jose, Rooster Rittmiller, and me.

We were already in the immediate area when I made the call. We had parked our bikes and proceeded on foot. When we got to the saloon, there was a massive crowd in front waiting to get in. Inside, the bar was filled to maximum capacity. As we stood at the back of the crowd, we saw two guys come out of the bar wearing their club cuts and red bandanas over their faces. One of them turned out to be an R&G enforcer. He was calling the shots for the moment. He started waving his arms and yelling at the crowd to get out of the way. It was like an out-of-body experience reminiscent of Moses parting the Red Sea. The crowd turned and looked at us as they parted the way, providing a clear, direct path for us straight to the front door.

The enforcer waved us forward and led us inside as the crowd watched. We were shown a place to stand and told to wait there. The place was packed! Several minutes passed and several bodyguard-type R&Gs escorted the Santa Fe president and his son to us. We noted the president was wearing a bulletproof vest under his cut. He greeted us with a kiss, which is a tradition with the R&G when they meet and greet someone they respect. It is a cultural thing within their club. It makes a silent statement of courtesy and acceptance. It can also appear as an endorsement to those watching the process.

The 1% outlaw clubs have protocols and requirements when blessing a new club into their world. By then I knew the process well. I also knew this club required new clubs wanting to run in their areas to wear an R&G "cookie." The cookie is what they call their "I Support the R&G" patch, which is to be worn on the front of your cut. They also have restrictions on acceptable colors of your back patch (club name and logo). We had a lot to talk about, and I remember again thinking (like many times before) how only God could get us through this complicated and detailed process. You can't appear cocky but must remain respectfully confident. And you can't blink or show even a hint of fear.

After the formal introductions, we got down to business. We did it right then and there, no office or special room, but right there on

The Red & Gold – Red River Part 1

our feet, surrounded by a buffer of R&Gs so the crowds of civilians couldn't eavesdrop. The R&G knew how to adapt, improvise, and get 'er done!

The first thing the Santa Fe president said to me was, "You guys came all the way from California just to see me?" He was smiling and expressed his gratitude and respect. After that, he looked me in the eye and said, "I want to know one thing: Are you guys real Christians?" I told him we were. He then said if we weren't, they would find out and it wouldn't go well for us. I told him if they ever had any problem with any of our members to call me first and I would resolve any issues immediately. I assured him we vet our members very carefully, but if any bad apples were to slip through, we would pull their patches immediately and send them packing.

Since I had the floor, I also told him we knew about their policy with cookies and couldn't wear them because we cross state lines doing God's business and we needed to remain supportive but independent, staying out of the politics as much as possible. He said, "Everybody has to wear our cookie, but you're exempt!"

I then said I understood outlaw protocol and how wearing a diamond patch (indicating outlaw biker status) can be an issue for the dominants, but ours were worn for a special reason. I explained how only 1% of the Christian biker clubs out there in the world could go where we go and do what we do.

The diamond patch is proprietary to most of the big 1%er clubs and if they see you wearing one you may get a gut check to see what you're made of. The outcome could be painful as well as embarrassing. The dominant clubs are known for physically overpowering you and cutting off any offensive patches in public. The more you resist their acts of dominance, the more painful things will get. Those guys play by their own rules. Some bikers who have demonstrated their intent of rebellion by flipping off an R&G member have been known to lose not only their patch (if they have one) but also their middle finger!

So again, while I still had the floor, I went on to say we had ten reasons for wearing diamonds (see below). I didn't list them all, but I told him Jesus is the most famous outlaw of all time and we were firmly in His camp. I also said we had broken all or most of God's Commandments and many of them daily. So, in God's eyes, we were all outlaws. Then I laid it out how 90% of our original members were ex-cons and had been there, done that. The president replied they don't allow any new clubs in their areas to wear diamonds. Then he said, "You're exempt!" Lastly, I mentioned our Black and White colors to which he said, "No one is allowed to wear Black and White colors here either… except you, you're exempt."

Then the national president from Texas stepped forward and asked me the same question the local president had first asked. I told him the same thing I told the local. And I told him he could hold me personally accountable if our club let them down anywhere on their turf. He said he would do so if we didn't do what we say we do and be who we say we are. He then came closer and shared how he had become a believer and was having Bible studies at his home. Go figure, I thought to myself!

Then the Santa Fe president said he thought New Mexico needed guys like us for spiritual support and all that comes with it. He further stated, "Wherever we are, you are welcome!" We were in! No concessions and no cookies. It was exhilarating! What was in it for them to take such a chance on us? God was in it for them, that's what, and He always goes before us to prepare the way. As the sit-down ended, we hung out for a while, making the rounds meeting and greeting.

With our mission complete, we rode back to California on angel's wings. We were on a natural high! There have been just too many miracles since we started up. Could all the remarkable occurrences we continued to experience simply be coincidence or luck? I think not! And this was just the beginning.

Below I've added the full reasons we wear a diamond patch on the front and back of our cuts. If you ever get a gut-check on the road someplace out of your territory, you better have a good answer.

- We wear a diamond out of respect for those who came before us. 90% of our co-founders were outlaws and ex-cons with extensive and impressive rap sheets.

- Also, some of our current members are ex-felons and former outlaws as well. They understand outlaw protocol and the rules of respect.

- We are a 1%er support ministry providing spiritual and humanitarian support. "We are here for you" and endeavor to be a blessing, not a curse!

- According to God's laws we are all outlaws who have broken all or most of His Commandments, and sometimes daily!

- Only 1% of the self-proclaimed Christian bikers out there can qualify for membership in our club.

- The diamond also represents Jesus to us. He was the original outlaw of His time in the eyes of society. He took our death sentence.

- The diamond is a reminder. We haven't forgotten our past sins against God and our fellow man. We don't judge others or think we are better than anyone else, just forgiven.

- Our club is a better fit for those who have an outlaw or rebellious past. Our members can best serve God in an environment natural and familiar to them. You can't take our guys and put them in a one-piece ministry patch, riding with gold wingers (folks who ride big Honda Gold Wing touring bikes). They just wouldn't fit in!

- We have broken out of the mold of our former lives as outlaws to the Word of God (notice how the borders of our diamonds are broken). We are an independent club (autonomous), here to help and support others.

- As "outlaws for Jesus," we come to fight injustice, Satan, and all that is evil.

Our club is our ministry. We are not a religious organization per se. We are a Christian men's MC. Our members are held to very high standards, and all are mature, born-again evangelicals. Considering their backgrounds, they would not fit very well with lighter-weight Christian clubs. There is nowhere for some of these guys to go. They are used to a hardcore lifestyle and learned to love the support, camaraderie, and brotherhood found in a club like ours. They like being held accountable and having structure in their lives. Our club becomes the family many of them have never had.

The Last Disciples MC is an independent club. We do not become involved in the politics of the biker subculture. We don't want to know other clubs' business and we will not be an exclusive support club or one showing favoritism only to certain clubs. Doing so would not be (in our opinion) the Christian way. We go where Jesus would go, seeking the lost wherever they are.

The Bible tells us to leave the ninety-nine who are safe and to go after the one that has gone astray (Matthew 18:12, NASB). That's what we do. If someone wants help with sobriety, program referrals, weddings, funerals, prayer for themselves, and/or prayer for their loved ones, we will be there for them.

18

RED RIVER PART II

SEVERAL YEARS LATER we ended up back in New Mexico. There is always more work to be done and we knew it would be good for our crew there if more of our other members showed up, not only to support them but also to support the R&G by attending another national run. While there I again ran into the R&G enforcer mentioned earlier. He told me how three years earlier, he was the one with the red bandana over his face who had parted the crowd for us at their national rally. He said from the moment he saw us, he realized he was in the wrong place for the wrong reasons, and we were in the right place for the right reasons.

He had served many years in prison for his club without ratting on his brothers. He had earned his place in the history of the club and was highly respected. You can use your imagination about what his job description entailed as an enforcer. He said his conscience had been tormenting him for some time. About two months before our current visit, he chose to formally opt out of the R&G, which is not usually an option with them. This put him in "bad standing" and a hit order was put out on him. His years of service as a club enforcer, working closely with national R&G business, had made him a security risk to the organization. He knew too much to just let him go.

It wasn't long before he had a surprise visit at his home from three lower-ranking club members who were hoping to gain status within the club by eliminating a problem. Often, the best defense is an offense, and as the former R&G enforcer threw open his front door he attacked them, beating down all three. As they started regaining their footing, he told them to go back and tell their boss to send five next time! He told me he was a former Navy SEAL and a high-degree black belt. He said his father had been a Special Forces hand-to-hand combat instructor and he (himself) had been training since he was a youngster. He had chosen not to run from the club, but to live in their midst. He is on fire for the Lord now and has placed all his faith and trust in Jesus. For several years afterward he stayed in touch with Jose.

By the grace of God, our helping and supporting the former enforcer has not affected our standing with the R&G to this day. I think much of this has to do with Jose's faithful visits and prayer vigils for downed R&G members over the years during medical crises, as well as for all the on-call help from our long-time brother Ain't Rite, who was always there to help. Ours is a spiritual and humanitarian mission, not a political one.

On this trip, to our surprise, the R&G Santa Fe president invited us to a private cabin deep in a valley near Red River. We never know what we are rolling into until we get there. Two presidents were there with their families and personal bodyguards along with their top trusted members. We were asked to hang out and break bread with them. After a great lunch and a careful discussion of MC politics, we asked to pray for the Santa Fe president's son.

His boy had come out on the bad end of a previous motorcycle accident. He received our prayers with enthusiasm as we prayed and anointed him with oil in the presence of all. We also witnessed to several others as the Holy Spirit led us. There is little or no leeway for error with words or protocol in this subculture. You can't look weak or appear cocky. Cool confidence must be apparent. This will suck the energy out of you because it's super intense! We were able to spend about an hour-and-a-half socializing at the cabin before rolling out to Red River for their national rally.

We had met up with our New Mexico representatives earlier and were now a spiritual force to be reckoned with. We split into two teams and worked the town, blessing people, visiting, witnessing, and giving out tracts as the Holy Spirit led us. I even shared with a couple of Jehovah's Witnesses, ladies who were sitting on a bench by the sidewalk. They both accepted one of our tracts. There were too many special moments to even try to record them all. All the dominant club members we encountered treated us with respect. Of course, we didn't limit our witnessing to only club members, any and all were fair game. One estimate was something like 25,000 people attended the rally over the three-day weekend, in a town consisting of not much more than a couple of main streets. A 2020 census showed a population of only 477 people.

On this trip, we encountered every weather condition except snow. We'd been through whiteouts before and prayed not to repeat that experience! We did manage to get caught in a hailstorm so severe I thought my face would bleed from the impact. It was unsafe for us to stop at the time and when I thought I couldn't take it anymore, I just began to laugh and yell out loud. I felt like a crazy man and I'm sure there are more than a few who would agree with that self-appraisal. And then it suddenly stopped, as quickly as it had started, and we rode out of it.

On one extremely windy leg of the trip, I hit a tie-down buckle that fell off a semi-truck with my front tire at about 75 mph. This broke the bead on my tire, but I was able to somehow ride into the Santa Fe Harley shop like I was riding on ice. I checked the pressure on my front tire, and it registered zero psi. No air. The tube had been destroyed on impact. I think there must have been angels holding up my 750-pound bike. Once my tire was fixed, we were back on the road.

The next day we were coming around a bend in the highway and came across a serious accident. There were four motorcycles in the roadway and the riders were slowing down oncoming traffic. One rider lay face-up on the pavement, a huge muscular guy who was unconscious. We all put our flashers on and parked on the shoulder to assist. Sandman, a nurse practitioner, and former trauma surgery assistant, opened his saddlebag and retrieved his stethoscope. He then went to work on the downed biker. The rider had not been wearing a helmet and an inexperienced member of his group cut him off and caused him to go into a slide and crash. The top of his shaven head looked like raw hamburger meat. It was horrific. We took over traffic control and Sandman stabilized the injured man until an ambulance arrived. Sandman was also a former corpsman when in the Navy and had seen his share of trauma cases.

Seeing those kinds of accidents is a sobering experience. It causes one to take an extra tug on their helmet strap, assuming you're wearing one. Although helmets are not required in New Mexico, I always wear a full-face now wherever I go.

On our last day, we attended a local church for much-needed praise and worship. Upon saying our goodbyes, the pastor put a donation of $341.31 in my hand as a love offering from his church.

Before returning home, I had an opportunity to share a very brief message of salvation with the Motel 6 manager where we stayed. I gave him a tract to back up what I shared with him. He said he would pray the prayer on the back of the card. With a little humor thrown in, I asked him, "Promise?" He smiled and said, "I promise."

He went on to say he would share it with his family too. It was the eve of his nephew's graduation and his whole family was gathering for the occasion. The next morning at about 5:00 am we were loading gear on our bikes for the trip home. The manager got my attention and told me his family wished to thank me for the prayer we sent with him to the festivities. He said he prayed the prayer out loud with his whole family as they stood in the backyard holding hands. Concealing my excitement, I asked casually how many of them had prayed the prayer with him. He said there were about thirty. Wow! It seems as if all we need to do is open our mouths and God will take care of all the rest! And that's exactly how it works. To Him be the Glory, all of it!

We pulled out of Espanola at 6:00 am and started our long trek home. We shared our faith and tracts with many along the way. Near a Navajo reservation in Arizona, we prayed for two Navajo Indians. One looked near death from alcoholism. The other seemed to have it together and was helping his friend. We blessed them with food money they had not asked for but gratefully accepted. I then felt compelled to pray for the sick one. We laid hands on him, and his companion also put a hand on his shoulder. I prayed what the Holy Spirit gave me to pray and then was led to a transition into the sinner's prayer. As we prayed for forgiveness for our sins and our belief in Jesus as our Lord and Savior, the Navajos began nodding their heads in affirmation. Before this, the sick one had been glassy-eyed and non-responsive. Only God knows their hearts, but I felt this was a divine appointment by the response and positive energy present.

We mounted up and pressed on. On our way home, we rode over a thousand miles in about twenty-one hours without sleep. We had to stop, stretch, coffee up, and refuel about every 150 miles. We may have stretched the speed limit a little to get home so quickly. But we were so energized we just kept on rolling! Sounds crazy, but we just laughed and yelled, "Hardcore for Jesus!" I got home at around 2:30 AM. My Harley looked like it had been to Hell and back. There was no doubt we were under the cover of spiritual protection and guidance all the way. Thank You, Lord!

19

Triple Homicide at Rio Rancho

One day I got a desperate call from New Mexico which motivated us to put out a prayer request for the surviving family members of a triple-homicide that had recently occurred on Father's Day in El Rancho, near Santa Fe. A father, mother, and their eighteen-year-old adopted son (who was partially blind, crippled, and mentally handicapped) were bludgeoned to death in their home with a pickaxe. All had been struck in the head and the handicapped boy reportedly had multiple wounds to the head.

Jose asked us to return to New Mexico for help ministering to the families and extended families of the victims. He said he didn't know what to say or do other than protect the family and make them feel safe. When I hung up, I remember thinking surely there was someone else in New Mexico to minister to the family. I took it to prayer and asked, "Why me, Lord?" I immediately heard a voice in my head saying, "Why *not* you?" I felt it was a directive from God, so I started planning. The next day two of us left California on our motorcycles and another left from Wyoming to meet us in Albuquerque. As we rode, we prayed for opportunities and divine appointments. Many tracts were given out along the way to people who mostly approached us with friendly questions. Those moments are always a blessing and encouragement.

Upon arrival, we found part of the victim's family lived in a mobile home only about fifty feet away from the house where the murders occurred. They had feared for their lives since the incident and had been supported by Jose from his first contact. He had made himself available for whatever they needed and had never left their side since the date it all went down. Jose was notably exhausted and wiped out physically, emotionally, and spiritually.

It took us two days to make the trip there. For the first couple of days we were there we talked with the police, surveyed the crime scene with permission, and ministered to the family and friends of the victims. We fellowshipped quite a bit in the mobile home next to the scene. On the second night, while the home was full of family, I took a break and went out back near the crime scene to just be still for a moment and pray. It was pitch black and very still. As I slowly paced, I felt another presence. It was one of the victim's daughters. She stepped out of the shadows and walked toward me. As I greeted her, she told me she knew we are supposed to forgive others, but she didn't think it would ever be possible for her. It was just too horrific. She also said she didn't think she could ever go back inside the family home.

I told her going inside the house was exactly what I thought she should do! I told her Satan wouldn't want her to forgive but would rather she struggle and suffer from agony and torment for the rest of her life. She told me I was probably right. The idea had come immediately. I had just prayed "Lord, why am I here? What can I do?" I told the young lady I didn't know if her family would agree to it, but I thought the best way to overcome their pain was to gather everyone together and go into their mom and dad's house and pray with me to rebuke the devil. I felt it would give them a release and set them free.

She immediately agreed and said she would talk with everyone. As I waited out back, a few minutes passed and then the whole family came out to hear me. I told them the true enemy was Satan. I also told them the house had been completely sanitized by the health department after the police investigation had been completed. The walls and ceiling had been washed and the carpets removed. Then I gave them the battle plan. They all looked at each other and agreed, "Let's do it!"

I went in first and turned on the living room light. Then everyone filed in solemnly. They were quiet and visibly nervous. I told them we should all hold hands in solidarity while I prayed. We all linked up and then the Holy Spirit spoke through me. I normally don't know what I'm going to say until I start praying. It just comes out if I trust in the Lord's guidance. I asked them to pray silently in agreement with me. I then prayed about Heaven and how, if we get there, we will see our loved ones again who went before us and how there will be nothing but beauty, peace, happiness, and the stunning glory of God's presence. It is a place where there will be no tears, no sorrow, no pain, and no suffering. Words cannot describe the grandeur.

I told them if we want to unite with our loved ones who we believe are in Heaven, then we had better make sure we were on the right path as well. I also told them if God forgave us and even died for us, we were also to forgive others. It was a choice we each must make, and if we want God's blessings, then we must strive to be obedient to Him. I told them Satan was the enemy of their souls and he wanted us to be under his control. He wanted us to suffer and curse God, but we have a choice. I also told them I was going to send a message to Satan. But first I explained the simple message of salvation and asked them all to repeat the sinner's prayer with me, publicly acknowledging Jesus as King of kings and Lord of lords, their Savior and Redeemer. I asked them to pray with all the sincerity they could muster, from their hearts. We then all prayed out loud together.

Next, I told them they now had power over Satan if they would just have faith and believe. I proceeded to rebuke Satan out loud, telling him the family was out of bounds and hands-off! I said he was to leave their minds alone and to leave the family home and their respective homes immediately because they were all now new creations in Christ, and he had no power over them. "Get out in the mighty name of Jesus!" I shouted.

Afterward, one of the in-laws came to me and said he had prayed and had never felt anything like it before, as if a current had run through him. Everyone has a different experience when they receive Christ. Some faint, some purge demons, and some just feel relief. But I believe everyone feels a sense of peace. I sure did.

After our prayer session, everyone was hanging around talking about it. The whole mood had changed. Pretty soon the guy who had talked to me afterward said his wife just arrived and he thought she would want to be a part of everything too. I told him to ask her. Pretty soon they came to me out back and I told her the message I had shared, and she agreed she wanted to receive Jesus too. So, we prayed together with her husband next to her. It was an amazing time. I think seven or more received Jesus that night.

After we wrapped things up, Sandman and I went to our motel to get some rest before the funeral the next day. I had told the family we would provide extra security and protection during the service in addition to the police who would also be present in plain clothes. The service was beautiful, and everyone seemed to be at peace.

Once back at our rooms, we packed up for our trip home in the morning. We were so happy about the outcome, and I then understood why I was supposed to be there. When God says "Go" we must be obedient! Blessings always seem to follow. God told Jonah (Jonah 1:3, NASB) to go to Nineveh, but he was afraid to go because he was a Hebrew and would be persecuted. So, he ran in the other direction and was swallowed by a great fish while at sea. After he was spat out onto the beach he obeyed and went where he was told. Through his preaching, the people turned back to God and the whole city was saved from God's wrath.

As we went out to our bikes for the trip home, we saw part of the extended family we had witnessed to the night before. They *happened* to be staying at the same motel because they were afraid to stay near the crime scene in case the killer returned. We greeted and hugged in the morning sun when I noticed a ten-year-old boy I hadn't met. I asked him if he had heard what we had done at his grandma and grandpa's house the night before. He said he had. So, I asked him what he thought about it.

He was a polite, quiet kid and very friendly. He volunteered he had recently gone to a local church with a neighboring family and how he liked it. He said it made him feel good. So, I asked if he wanted to pray the same prayer his parents had prayed with us. He enthusiastically said yes. Sandman and I, along with the boy's family, all laid hands on him as he repeated the sinner's prayer, asking Jesus to come into his life. When you think about the sequence of events above, how could you *not* believe in miracles?

20

THE BLACK & WHITE

AFTER STARTING THINGS up for the Last Disciples in California and New Mexico, inquiries started coming in from all over. We had a website up and running from the beginning and the networking was flowing. Where would the next sit-down be? We knew if we were to survive our endeavor we would need to hook up with the Black & White Nation, an international club considered among the top five 1%er clubs in the US.

Again, we put the word out on the streets. Within a week we got a message back from our source that the Black & White were "good with us." This made me a little nervous and I sent a message back saying I wanted to meet with a club officer in person instead of relying on relayed messages through a third party. We hadn't come this far by assuming things! To keep our brothers safe, I wanted to have an in-person meeting so we would have a name, date, and location to fall back on if challenged somewhere on the road. But after two attempts we got no further reply.

So, after careful deliberation, we decided to establish a SoCal chapter. We already had vetted members there who had been flying blacked-out (without patches, wearing plain black cuts). They got patched up and began attending all the "open" functions in their area. On one of their first runs they rolled into a rally without first scouting out the venue beforehand. They parked, dismounted, and began looking around. Then it dawned on them that they were in a sea of Black and White bikers, and they were being stared at. Our SoCal president and his crew started walking toward a big guy they thought to be the leader. Immediately they were surrounded by the outlaw club, and they weren't smiling. Two huge Sergeants-at-Arms stepped in front of their leader ready to protect him as their other brothers formed a wall of impenetrable tattooed and leathered flesh.

The moment was tense as time momentarily froze. All became quiet, and then a loud voice said; "Let 'em through." It was the SoCal president of Black and White. As our representatives moved forward they met the officer who extended his hand to our local president. He then said; "I know who you are, we checked you guys out and we're good with you. Now turn your backs to the crowd so they can see your patch." He then said to his club brothers and all the onlookers, "We're good with these guys, nobody touches them." After the introduction our guys were greeted and made welcome. We were formally in.

Not long afterward, we again heard from our contact about a fundraiser being put on by the Black & White MC in California City. That was an opportunity to follow through and support their cause, which was a worthy one. You can't just show up unless they have invited you or unless you have already been approved to fly in their areas. Patience and persistence paid off. It's amazing how God has never failed us. The event was being held at a local VFW hall.

The reason for the fundraiser was due to a federal lawsuit levied against the Black & White MC's trademark, as represented by their name and logo. Since it was a registered trademark and the club had members who had been indicted and convicted for racketeering, under the "RICO Act" (racketeer influenced and corrupt organizations), the feds thought they had a good case against them. They wanted to shut them down by seizing their trademark and outlawing any future use.

Now granted, bikers have always been known for being on the rebellious side. Some chapters, or individual members of some clubs, can be criminally motivated, but there are also thousands of club members and chapters and clubs who do not fall under the purview of the RICO Act. What about them? It was like a basic freedom was being chipped away at. I think most people today feel like our government of, by, and for the people is getting too big and clumsy.

This take-the-patch process could lead to a slippery slope with other clubs, eventually causing the same thing to happen to any MCs who had members busted for personal crimes, even if the crime had nothing whatsoever to do with actual club business. New laws could surface, and as a result motorcycle clubs could even be banned. Sound far-fetched? It is already happening in Australia as I write this! We are in the loop on this since we now have members there.

Due to Black & White's charges for unlawful trademark use, the biker community at large was drawn to support all the outlaw MCs in their quest to *save the patch*. And that's how we got connected. We had voted to attend the fundraiser as a way of not only supporting a cause that could affect our rights regarding freedom of expression and assembly, but it was also a way to meet the Black & White and to represent our endeavor to promote the Last Disciples MC.

Time flew by and we were soon on the road to California City. It was a beautiful, warm, and sunny day, which I can only describe as heavenly. Perfect riding weather! There were five of us national officers representing our MC. By now we were getting more security conscious. So, upon our arrival, we stopped about a mile out. I sent in a scout to do a quick drive-by to assess the situation. I wanted to know if anything looked hinky, what other clubs might be there, where we would enter and park, and so on. It's just a good thing to do, especially when you only have a five-man crew with you! We wanted to look sharp as we rode in.

The intelligence came back good, and everything looked straight up. As we rolled up to the back entrance of the VFW Hall we were directed by a Black & White prospect where to line up our bikes. He also told us if we had any guns or knives on us to leave them in our saddlebags. The entire area was surrounded by chain-link fencing and lots of prospects were there for security. As we approached the back entrance from the parking area we were met by full-patch members who used metal detectors to scan us for weapons, just to be sure we had followed their instructions.

Next, we had to pay for our meals, which was the only support asked of us. The person collecting funds at the time was a massively muscular guy wearing a president tag. He was the kind of guy you don't forget. He was covered in tats. He even had a Harley Davidson logo tattooed on the top of his head. As I paid him for my meal ticket, he thanked me. I told him who I was and visited a little to break the ice. I then reached into my cut and withdrew an envelope containing a $100 bill and handed it to him. As he opened it to look inside, I said, "Just a little extra for the cause." He was surprised and grateful.

As we met many of the people inside the hall, I realized there were some surprisingly famous legends present. For one, I recognized a former SAA (sergeant-at-arms) named "Red Dog." He had been featured in the book *Under and Alone* by an Alcohol, Tobacco and Firearms (ATF) infiltrator named William Queens. The place was too packed to be able to meet everyone.

One member approached me and thanked us for showing up. His name was Repo, and he was an actor when he wasn't riding with the club. Also, another came forward and introduced himself as the new B&W national president. Amazing! Our invitation to the event was very timely and it opened yet another door for us.

The Black & White

As we sat down to eat, more members would walk up to our table and introduce themselves, thanking us for our support. One member introduced himself and asked me if we were the ones who kicked in the extra bucks. I acknowledged we were, and he expressed his appreciation and sincere gratitude. To this day I feel it was one of the best donations we ever made. The cause was worthy and another possible barrier was being overcome.

Little did I know at the time how years later I would provide the local president (who I met at the front door upon our arrival) with spiritual counsel when he needed help. I also would do a baby dedication near San Francisco for him and his new wife's first child. We became friends and one day I sent him one of our sinner's prayer tracts which he prayed with his adopted mother when she lay on her death bed. I had told him it would make her smile when they prayed together, and it did. He has since left the club life and is embracing his faith and new sobriety. He became an entrepreneur, marketing his designs of gym accessories. He was formerly an MMA competitor and an arm-wrestling champion, competing one year at the Arnold Schwarzenegger Classic. We are still in touch and good friends to this day. He recently asked me if I would baptize him the next time we meet. I assured him I would!

21

Laughlin River Rallies

OVER THE YEARS we had settled on making annual runs to Laughlin, Nevada for their Annual River Run. It seemed as if each time we went there, people were getting saved, which is what it's all about. Back in 2002 the R&W and the B&W clubs had a run-in at the Harrah's Laughlin Casino on the main strip. It led to three deaths. One club member was stabbed to death and two others were shot and killed.

After the incident, the casinos in Laughlin banned the wearing of club patches while on casino property. Even T-shirts with club names were banned to prevent another incident. This eventually caused a boycott of the River Run by many notable clubs. The exhibits and entertainment were all set up on casino properties. About all you could do was wear your colors while riding through town. That kind of took the wind out of the sails of the River Run for a lot of participants and club support groups. Nonetheless, we still went there. We would ride in with our cuts on, park, and lock our colors in our saddlebags.

Our approach was to wear black and white clothing without a stitch of another color. This way we could be recognized as a club but without flashing the patches. People always seem to be interested in the real MCs. As we engaged people in conversations, we would tell them who we were. They would then have lots of questions. We were always able to give out lots of tracts, which were always accepted and never turned back. We had the best quality tracts money could buy. They looked classy and had a biker cartoon on the front with text that reads: "Life's two most important questions: If you died today are you certain you would go to Heaven? And if God said why should I let you in? What would your answer be?"

Those questions always intrigued those who read them. Almost all of them would say, "Well, I'm a good person and I've done more good than bad." Then we would have them turn the card over and they would see the verse from Romans that says, "There are none righteous, no not one, for all fall short of the Kingdom of God" (Romans 3:10, NKJV). As their countenance would begin to fade, we'd ask them to read on. Because next, the card goes on to say there is good news because "Everyone who calls on the name of the Lord will be saved" (Romans 10:13 NASB). This in turn leads them to the sinner's prayer. Over all the years I have been handing out these cards, I've only had three people hand it back and say no thanks. But I can rest assured I had done my part as a messenger of Jesus Christ. It must be done with gentleness, love, and reverence.

We have used this technique not only with the outlaw bikers but with anyone we were drawn to, including motel maids, management, waitresses, service station employees, you name it. God wants none to be lost and neither do we. We always leave new converts with a couple extra tracts, our contact information, and a new Biker Bible. As I've said elsewhere in these writings, everyone is fair game. Now it's up to you. Challenge yourself to lead just one soul to salvation during your lifetime. It's like that old Frito-Lay commercial from the 1960s that said, "Betcha can't eat just one!" Cookies from Heaven are just like that. Once you have one, you just can't stop. Happy Hunting!

22

Las Vegas Tension

As our organization grew, I got a call one day from a guy who was an ex-con living in Las Vegas. He told me he was interested in joining up. He said his son was also interested and that he might have a few other guys as well. I put him through our usual screening procedure over the phone. He told me he got himself on the right track while in prison and was now an ordained pastor. I'd heard this more than a time or two before and usually take it with a grain of salt. But after talking for about an hour, I felt this guy might be a viable candidate for our vetting process. So, I offered him an application and told him the process could take up to a year. He assured me he was good with that.

After taking the time it takes to vet a new guy, he was looking pretty good. He had to contact and introduce himself to all our national officers and subject himself to their scrutiny as well. His wife was also interviewed as was his son and all the references listed on his application. Next, he was required to take our Discipleship Program to ensure our beliefs were in sync. Then he had to hang around areas frequented by the dominants. He had to wear black and white clothing and a plain black leather vest without a single patch of any kind attached. It's a period of submission and humbling any serious candidate goes through. We did the same with his 400-pound son, who I will call "Dumpster." As I recall, the kid wore size seventeen shoes. He had to have them custom-made. He was so huge he couldn't even fit on a motorcycle. Instead, we gave him special permission to ride his VW Trike. There was just no other way.

As the father-son team jumped through all the hoops, the day finally came when their vetting was complete and it was time to take a yea or nay vote on the burly duo. They got the vote and were patched in. There was just one little detail. To fly an MC patch in Nevada, you had to be cleared through the local COC (Confederation of Clubs). At the time, Las Vegas had two dominants who shared the turf. The R&W and the B&W. So, in this case, there were two COCs, which meant we had to get into both to get blessed-in to fly.

The pastor had some connections, and we thankfully got the invites. It just so happened both COCs had their meetings on the same day, at different hours. For the formalities, we brought in our New Mexico Rep. He stood about six feet tall and weighed in at around 285 pounds. He was fearless, bulletproof, and confident. We prayed up, then our Rep arrived, and after representing us tactfully, both COCs voted in the affirmative. He had a command presence they respected. Things just fell into place, yet we overcame tremendous odds once again. Hardly a coincidence!

After the dust settled in Vegas, I got a call one day at our California headquarters. It was the Vegas pastor. He said, "Lou, we've got a problem. We're on the main Vegas strip and just got pulled over by a crew of B&W and they're not happy. They ordered us to take off our colors or they will cut them off us. What do we do?" The pastor went on to say the crew leader who was doing all the talking was wearing a president tag.

I told him not to remove his colors but to stand firm. I then asked him to put the president on the phone. He tried to hand it off, but the guy said "[expletive] no" in a most aggressive manner. I told the pastor to tell the guy that talking with me was the only way to peacefully resolve the issue. The president was furious but agreed. He snatched the pastor's cell phone and yelled, "You better have the right answers or we're going to cut those [expletive] colors off, right here, right now! We've got guys who died for that Diamond!"

A calm confidence came over me I can't explain. I told the president, "Friend, you need to take a deep breath and listen to me for a minute. Nobody's cutting anybody's patches off."

He said, "Okay, talk." I then told him we had followed protocol to the letter and only a month or so ago we had attended both COCs in Vegas by invitation. I went on to say how members from his chapter were present at the meeting and how we had been voted in unanimously. I also related to him how we had been originally blessed-in by his club in southern California, by a president named "House" (may he rest in peace). House came about his name based on his size because he was "as big as a house." He had passed away in jail when the corrections staff failed to give him his life-supporting medication. Not too many people would know those details.

The Las Vegas president then said, "You better be telling the truth, or somebody's gonna pay. Call me back in ten minutes!" Then he hung up. I immediately made a call to the B&W president we had met in California City at the VFW fundraiser. He picked up right away and I gave him an abbreviated account of what was going on. He then said he'd call me back in five. I don't know who he talked to, but he called me back right away and said we should be good to go.

When I called back to Vegas the president answered in a happy tone, saying, "Hey man, I just talked to SoCal and it's all good!" He went on to relate how he had missed the COC meeting and just hadn't been filled in yet. After we hung up, the Vegas B&W crew introduced themselves to our guys, shook hands, and gave them hugs. They then invited our guys to lunch, on them. The situation had gone from dire to peaceful in just ten minutes! Once again, God was watching our six. Thank You Lord!

23
THE BLUE & WHITE

BACK ON HOME turf, we had been invited to a barbecue at the Black & Gold MC clubhouse in Atascadero. We had been told that a 1%er club who wear Blue & White would be there. They are a big California outlaw club. When we arrived, we were greeted by the B&G who told us the "Double Ds" (Blue and White) were already there and everyone was anticipating a possible blowup. The reason was because we both used a similar name on our top rockers which are sewn above the center patch. They were the 1%ers, and we were the new club on the block. So, I motioned our sergeant-at-arms over and told him the deal and to gather our guys together and bring them to me.

It was a beautiful day and about ten of the Blue and Whites were sitting outside the clubhouse at the picnic benches chowing down. That was good because it gave us the upper hand (at least psychologically) as we approached in a group. I had told our guys to keep it loose and friendly. As they saw us coming, they all jumped to their feet not knowing what was next.

I had already picked out the boss, and I smiled as I approached him, introduced myself, and stuck out my hand. They received us warmly with handshakes and shoulder bumps all-round. Whew! They treated us as brothers and invited us to come down to Los Angeles for a memorial celebration and BBQ at their clubhouse. All I could think was "How cool is that?" We just never know what we may be walking into. It's a rough and tumble world, but our goal is always to love people, not to fight them. God always seems to go before us to prepare the way for peace.

We accepted their invitation and made the trek south the following weekend, a 200-mile ride one way. While there we made lots of contacts and were treated like family by all. The biker ministry the Lord brought me into has proven to be the most exciting and challenging venue I could have ever pursued. What a blessing! I was receiving exactly what I had prayed for. The adrenaline can really pump at times when we walk by faith and not by sight. Glory to God!

24

Reno Shootout

On one of our annual runs to the Street Vibes regional rally in and around Reno, Nevada, we were visiting one of the local hot spots, John Ascuaga's Nugget Casino in Sparks. Vendor booths were everywhere as is the custom. There were thousands of bikers and a variety of clubs present. As we were making our rounds, everything was going as normal. One of the first things we usually do is to seek out the big-name clubs so we can stop by and pay our respects. As we strolled about, we ran into a crew of Greens near an R&W booth.

We greeted them and they were a little cool at first. They asked who we were and where we were from and if we were wearing any support flash from another club who might not be on friendly terms with them. I kept it light and easy and told them we don't wear support patches. They then loosened up and we made a little small talk. We said our goodbyes and walked over to the R&W booth where they were selling T-shirts, hats, and so on. There we met the HA president, Jeff Pettigrew, from San Jose, California. The atmosphere was friendly, and all went well.

We wandered around a while, meeting folks and sharing tracts. Not long after leaving the HA's booth, we got word someone had shot and killed the R&W president we had just been talking to (may he rest in peace). The word traveled quickly throughout the rally. Reportedly, approximately twenty shots had been fired, but we never heard them. With the help of our sergeant-at-arms, I summoned our crew to a predetermined location and we rolled out of town. The next day there was a retaliatory shooting, killing a member of the rival club involved in the shootout. The weekend turned out to be a dangerous fiasco. As I said previously, you never know!

25

SAN JOSE SHOOTOUT

ABOUT A MONTH after the shooting, we received an invitation to attend the funeral service for the R&W president who had been killed in Sparks. Jeffrey "Jethro" Pettigrew's funeral service was to be held at a cemetery chapel in San Jose. He had reportedly been shot in the back four times.

It was another picture-perfect day as we rolled northbound from Paso Robles to San Jose for the service. When we arrived at the chapel there were masses of bikers everywhere who had come to pay their respects. We parked together in a uniform row, as usual, then mixed through the crowd and made our way to the chapel. As we walked inside there were R&Ws strategically placed for security. The interior was set up as you would expect in any church, with the casket up front by the altar. It was beautifully painted in gleaming white with bold red flames and pinstriping. As I stood in the foyer with our Sacramento chapter president, Iron Mike, a steady flow of bikers came in, moving slowly toward the open casket and then out an exit near the front.

As they filtered in, I recognized an R&W I had met several times before while visiting one of their chapters. As he started to pass by us, I called out his name and to my surprise, he quickly turned toward me and put his nose in my face, about two inches away. He then said he had seen me on the internet with my arm around one of their enemies. As mentioned earlier, because we are

Christians, we make every attempt to remain out of the politics between clubs.

I told him so, and how it was unlikely the person he saw me with in the picture was, in fact, their enemy, since I avoid being photographed in situations that could cause anyone heartburn. Through the obscenities and accusations, I stood my ground and maintained eye contact, which was all I could do. We were in very tight quarters. He then told me we were not welcome there and we needed to leave.

I told him before we could do so he needed to check first with the four HA presidents who had invited us and made us welcome at the service. I also pointed out how one of the biggest bouquets in the chapel was a memorial gift from us. Unbeknownst to him, I had also previously met Jethro's daughter inside and gave her a $200 check from our club to help their family out. He then started drifting inward with the crowd while still staring me down. He then walked forward to the casket to pay his respects.

I was not happy with the rude treatment. Traditionally, it's not cool to cause an altercation at biker funerals or memorials. The older bikers who have been around the block know this. When Mike and I walked outside, I looked for the angry R&W member. I also located another R&W to whom I had ministered for years. We were friends and I knew I could talk to him about anything. He had been with the R&W for over twenty years at the time. He was ticked off when I told him what had happened. He said he would talk with the guy and we should stay put and not leave. I saw him again about fifteen minutes later and he said all was good. Soon after, I saw the angry guy in the crowd again and worked my way over to him. I told him we needed to talk. He blew me off and said we didn't have anything to talk about as he walked away with a prospect. I said, "Okay, fine," and let it go.

After we had paid our respects and mingled with the crowd for a while, we gathered up our guys and rode to a local Starbucks. While there we got a call saying there had just been a shooting at the chapel right after we left. As it turned out, two R&Ws standing right where we had just stood got into an argument. One of them pulled a gun and killed his clubmate. This happened before Jethro had even been lowered into the ground.

The next day I found the news story was already online and knew exactly who the shooter was. I remembered seeing him inside the chapel. He had his cut snapped up to the neck and had his arms folded over his chest. I remembered thinking at the time he was armed. Yup, he was! Life is fleeting. We can be alive one second and dead the next. That's why we do what we do. We try to save every soul we can since no one is guaranteed a tomorrow. Are you ready? Or do you maybe know someone you need to share your faith with while they're still around? Sobering thought!

26
The Phoenix 81 Connection

By now we had chapters and nomad members scattered around the US, Australia, and Canada. I should note that "nomad" members are those who are not attached to a chapter yet or are in a new area waiting to gather enough members to form one. In 1%er clubs, nomads are often used to "take care of problems."

We had a good brother named "Reaper" in Albuquerque who was planning a job-related move to Phoenix, so we started planning and praying for God's divine will. As word started to spread about us having a couple of guys living in the Phoenix area, with another one on the way, word filtered back to us we were not going to be able to fly there, like ever. We had heard it all before, but things always changed and went in our favor in each case.

R&W is the dominant club in the Phoenix area. They are bordered by about a half-dozen counties. Just because one of their chapters lets you in doesn't mean the others will. They are autonomous in this regard. Phoenix is a complex of club jurisdictions but with R&W calling the shots. I told Reaper we had heard the word "never" a time or two and to just follow protocol and do what we do. When someone would say "never" I would always respond with a laugh and say, "To know us is to love us." That always used to lighten things up a little.

As we did our research, we got the name of the HA Phoenix president. We continued to give it to God, asking that *His* will be done, and if He opened the door, we would walk through it. As it turned out, Reaper was able to talk to the president on the phone, which in itself was not the easiest thing to accomplish. As Reaper, who is easy-going and amiable, small-talked to break the ice, the president said he had grown up in Wyoming. Then Reaper told him his wife came from Wyoming. As they compared notes, it turned out Reaper's wife had gone to high school with the guy. Now again I must ask, what are the odds of this happening in a country the size of the USA? I was beginning to think we should just spend our dues money on lottery tickets and then give all the winnings to the poor! God surely had His hand on us once again.

During the conversation, the president invited him to their clubhouse for an upcoming barbecue. Reaper represented for us with "Doc" and another couple of our local guys who were all made welcome. By the end of the feast, we were in. Just like that! Again, all we had done was to include the Lord in all our planning. "Thy Kingdom come, Thy will be done, Lord!" It was another one of those miracles folks so often call a coincidence.

After the bless-in, our Last Disciples brothers started attending everything happening in the greater Phoenix area. But as word got around that the Phoenix R&W chapter was good with us, we started getting word we still weren't welcome in Cave Creek, Yuma, and some other 81 strongholds in the area, despite the Phoenix green light. But, as always, we kept giving it up to the Lord. "If God is for us, who can be against us?" (Romans 8:31, NIV). Works for me! We walk by faith, praying we are within God's will, and trying not to get ahead of Him. Remember; "He must increase but I [we] must decrease" (John 3:30, NASB).

As we went about our work in Arizona, within two months the other R&W Chapters gave us the nod. We were good to go, or at least according to dominant club protocol that's the way it's *supposed* to work. But then our guys went to yet another biker run and ran into a club I will leave unnamed. Our brothers spotted them and walked over for a meet and greet. The reception was less than warm but civil. They then warmed up a little and invited our brothers to walk over to their tattoo booth down by the river. Our guys accepted and were led on a "shortcut" through some desert brush.

As soon as they got out of sight from the public, about a dozen bikers came out of the brush where they had been concealed and surrounded our four members. As some put their hands on their knives, they ordered our brothers to take off their cuts. Well, this wasn't the Last Disciples' first challenge, and they were prepared. It is legal to carry firearms on your person in Arizona and our guys were all armed. One was a combat veteran, and the others had a handle on the 1% lifestyle. Reaper himself had been stabbed twice years prior when he was a member of an outlaw club before getting saved. It became a Mexican standoff. Reaper said "No," and things got down to the nitty-gritty. The posse chose to back down before bullets and knives were put into action. The challengers said our guys could leave but if they saw them again wearing their patches "it would be on!"

When our guys got back to their bikes, Reaper called me. I told him to knock the dust off their boots, keep their cuts on, and ride out as they rode in, which they did. They later called the HA president and brought him up to date. The president said he knew the guys who confronted them and said he would take care of it. Not long afterward there was another run-in with the same guys who had ambushed our crew by the river. But it was at the HA clubhouse, and although everyone stood down, there was definite tension in the air.

For a while, it seemed like things were mellowing out. It got to the point where our guys thought the whole fiasco was squashed.

They heard the club that had bushwhacked them was hosting an "open house" fundraiser. The word was that everyone was invited. Reaper and his crew discussed it and thought it would be a good opportunity to support their cause and mend fences. But when they walked into the main room of the clubhouse the sergeant-at-arms burst into the room with a gun in each hand saying, "This [expletive] is gonna stop and it's gonna stop right now!" Again, when challenged, our guys refused to take off their colors.

Reaper later told me of the intensity. One of our war veterans was planning out in his mind the order in which he was going to take the enemy out. But once again the enemy relented, and our guys walked out. They met at the bikes and discussed finding a way, as Christians, to make things right. So, several of them removed their cuts and locked them in their saddlebags, and walked back inside, leaving one man outside to watch their bikes. To their surprise, they were cheered and embraced with hugs. After all, they were in another club's clubhouse and protocol dictates the club owning the clubhouse can invite other patches across their threshold, or not. It's their house and it's up to them. Nothing should be assumed. Our guys later mounted up with their colors back on and again rode off as they had ridden in.

Reaper had made it clear to them that his crew would be flying our patch on the road wherever they went. As it turned out I recommended we continue to fly anywhere we were made welcome and to just avoid the club that wouldn't accept us. And that's the way it remains today. The president of that club and Reaper had a cordial phone conversation after things cooled down a little. That was a plus. Hey, what can I say? Things get gnarly sometimes! If it was easy everyone would be doing it, right? Every time I tell some of our war stories someone always says; "Man, you should write a book!"

Lou Steel

My wife Reann

Teenage gunslingers, author on left, Robert Morgan (R.I.P.) on right.

My new 2001 Harley Dyna

Our first chapter at Morro Bay, California.

Author at Sturgis, South Dakota.

Lou Steel in New Mexico.

Ninja at Red River, New Mexico.

Brother Chapo, Cofounder (R.I.P.)

Robert "Chapo" Garcia (R.I.P.)

Ninja, Int'l President

Danny Blade, Nat'l SAA

Skeeter, Nat'l Secretary

Nitro, Vice President, Illinois

Animal, West Region President

Sandman, Texas Rep.

Sandman

Author and son Ryan.

On the road, L to R, Chapo and Pat.

L to R, Pat and Captain.

Motel Maid Kassandra, Laughlin, Nevada, accepts Jesus.

Author sharing with Jehovah's Witnesses.

Last Disciples crew in Colorado.

LDMC crew rolling through Colorado.

Stan the Man, aka Rocky.

L to R, Ninja, Nitro, and Cinco, in Illinois.

Joe "Magic" Perez, National Chaplain, in Albuquerque, New Mexico.

L to R, Ninja and Magic.

Trash, Nomad – Arkansas

Ninja, Int'l President, Aurora, Illinois.

Lou Steel aka Raven, Cofounder, National Nomad.

Tick Tock, Florida Rep.

LDMC crew taking a break.

Last Disciples 2021 National Run

Stev Morley, Australia Nat'l Rep.

LDMC "Black Ops" Aussie Crew, L to R -Eagleye Mike, Chopper, Skidz, Macka, Charlie.

27

Massaging the Spirit

Due to some sporadic back and neck pain, I had been seeing a local chiropractor. The adjustments usually left me worse off than before, so the doc decided I might benefit from massage therapy. I started seeing Kelly, his massage therapist. Each time, she would have me lie face down on the table with my face looking through the little padded hole in the headrest. It was an awkward way to converse, but I didn't have much choice. It was an even more awkward way to witness to someone, but I was nonetheless willing. I ended up sharing my testimony and the Bible with Kelly frequently. I had even given her one of our sinner's prayer tracts, but she wasn't ready.

One day, I had been preparing to fly back east to visit my sister in Virginia. I had lots to do and was feeling overwhelmed as the hours counted down to departure. When my phone rang, I was surprised to hear the voice of the receptionist at the chiropractor's office. She reminded me I had an appointment in twenty minutes. I was on the verge of canceling but then remembered Kelly. What if today was her day? I told the receptionist I would be right in. I knew this could be more important than anything I had planned for myself. On the way, I prayed I would not get ahead of the Spirit and if I were to speak, the Lord would give me the words and speak through me. With Kelly, I had already exhausted every Bible verse and testimony I could think of. What would I say if I were to speak at all?

As I reached for the doorknob of the doctor's office, I said "Amen." When I saw Kelly, she was all smiling and happy. After all, it happened to be Christmas Eve day. As we went through the procedure and I flopped face down on the table again, I began to pray to myself. We only exchanged a few words of small talk when I simply blurted out; "Kelly, did you ever pray the prayer on the little card I gave you?"

She replied, "No, I'm just not ready, I have some issues in my life." I then told her I had given her the best I have. I told her I didn't have anything more. I went on to tell her how God brings me to people and uses me to tell them about His love and saving grace. I told her I had been coming all those months more for her than for myself because I felt the Lord had led me to do so.

Then I told her, "Kelly, Jesus loves you just as you are right now, today. He knew, before either of us were even born, whether you would accept or deny Him. This may be my last visit and I just wanted to tell you Jesus loves you." Kelly started crying. I thought at first that maybe she had a cold or allergies. I looked up to see the torment on her face and knew she was truly broken inside.

I sat up on the massage table and asked her if she wanted to ask Jesus into her heart and she said yes not once but twice. We prayed together and she wept like a child who had just found her daddy after being lost and scared for a long time. She hugged me and sobbed. I could hardly control my tears of joy. Kelly then told me as she wiped away her tears how she didn't think Jesus could forgive her for her sins because she had an ongoing "issue."

I told her Jesus would fix it for her if she asked Him to and trusted in Him. As it turned out, I kept returning for therapy on my beat-up back and neck. Each time I would feed Kelly with Bible verses and stories of my ministry escapades. Then one day she said she needed to tell me what her sin was that had been haunting her.

I told her I didn't need to know but she insisted. I will keep it confidential, but it was such a small thing!

Satan had used it to convince her she wasn't acceptable to Jesus. Since we prayed that day, Kelly had reunited with her estranged mother, and they were planning to buy a house together. The last time I saw her she told me her reconciliation with her mother had seemed impossible before Jesus came into her life. She had told her mom about Jesus and they soon decided they were going to have a God-centered home and life together. Ain't that something!

28

Black & Gold Memorial

After the death of a local club member, we were invited to attend the funeral service. He was a member of the Black & Gold. They have chapters spread throughout California. Their deceased brother had been subdued during an arrest for a warrant by four deputy sheriffs whose combined weight had suffocated the guy. There were more than 200 bikers at the funeral. Tension and emotions ran high.

The service was officiated by Pastor Dick, a local pastor. He did a great job of walking a tough line, showing support for the despondent club members and family, but also urging order to be kept and the justice system to be given a chance to work. He also gave a message of salvation, and at the end asked any whose hearts were touched by the service to contact one of the Christian clubs present.

After the service, we rolled *en masse* to the fundraiser to follow at a local bowling alley ten miles to the north. Two hundred Harleys took to the freeway in a show of rolling thunder. The highway patrol tried to keep traffic out of our way by blocking on-ramps and overpasses. It must have been quite a spectacle to behold as an outsider.

When we got to the bowling alley, a guy I'll call Jerry (who was a member of my old HOG chapter) came over to talk. I had shared a little of my faith with him several times in the past, ever so gently. But that day he seemed hungry for more. As I shared with him, I would quote or paraphrase the Bible as best I could. He then asked if I would come over to his house sometime to talk with him and his family about Jesus. A Christian lady friend who overheard us talking motioned to me and said, "You guys need to go out in the parking lot and pray."

Jerry, overhearing her, enthusiastically said, "Okay, let's do it." The three of us walked outside under a big shady oak tree and Jerry simply dropped to his knees! Right in front of all the bikers in the parking lot. It caught me a little off guard. But we took a knee also and laid hands on Jerry's shoulders. After I explained the Gospel message, we all bowed our heads and prayed the sinner's prayer, with Jerry tearfully repeating every word.

As we were praying, I became aware of another close presence. Two legs had appeared next to Jerry. It caught me off guard and I felt vulnerable for a moment. I wanted to look up but didn't. I kept praying. When we all said "Amen," I saw it was a lady in jeans. She had also placed a hand on Jerry. She was smiling as she gently patted him on the back and walked away without a word. We all looked at each other in wonderment and Jerry, wiping his nose said, "That was my guardian angel." None of us had ever seen her before or since. It was a very special moment, as Jerry became a new creation in Christ.

He later told me he had been waiting for the right person to lead him to faith. Unbeknownst to me, he said he had been watching me for two years, knowing I was a Christian. He said I was walking what I was talking and that's how he decided I was the one. I was surprised and humbled.

The moral of this story is how we never know who is watching us. If we are preaching Christ, and Him crucified, we had better be good ambassadors! As followers of Jesus do we behave the same regardless of the circumstances? We must be "real," or we may be the cause of a lost soul! Some plant, some water, and some harvest. We never know where each person is in their spiritual journey. Jerry grew fast in his faith and wanted to help others who are battling addictions.

I discovered recently how the seed we had planted that day had taken root and flourished. Jerry had since become a member and chaplain of the Black Sheep Motorcycle Ministry. We must always be prepared to give a reason for the hope in our hearts. Our responsibility is great and may echo into eternity!

# 29
Street Vibes – Reno, NV

Street Vibrations or "Street Vibes" is a large secular motorcycle rally hosted in Reno, Nevada as I mentioned previously in Chapter 24. I prayed for safety before leaving home, asking the Lord to help us to recognize any divine appointments. I met up with my road buddy Sandman in Fresno and we rode to Reno together. It was a great ride, and the weather was perfect. On the way, we stopped somewhere south of Stockton, California for gas. We couldn't find a name-brand station and were led around and about a little town until we finally stumbled upon a Chevron station with a Mini-Mart.

We fueled up and used the restrooms. A Hindu girl was working the register inside. She saw our Harleys and told Sandman how she heard "Harley people" make the best meth. He said we were Christians and told her all about the horrors meth, and drugs in general, bring into the lives of users. The girl laughed and said she had never heard of "Harley Christians."

When I came out of the restroom, she was smoking by the front door. I said hi to her and a conversation started up again about "Christian Harley people." When I had a chance, I asked her about her beliefs. She named a few Hindu gods I had never heard of and told me it was a sin for them to believe in Jesus. With the impact of this idea, I was struck speechless and was given no words for her. Perhaps the expression on my face was sufficient for the moment.

We returned to our bikes and were soon approached by a guy dressed in station attendant clothing. He was the janitor named Henry. He was laughing about a conversation he just had with the Hindu girl. She likewise told him she had never heard of "Christian Harley people" and he seemed to get a kick out of it too. I told the guy there were many of us around and asked him if *he* knew anything about our Jesus.

He said he knew who Jesus was but that was about it. He then changed the subject and began to pour out the miseries and problems of his life. I told him I used to have the same concerns and problems, but Jesus showed me another way and set me free. I then proceeded to tell him who Jesus really is and what He did for us, and for me personally. I quoted and paraphrased some scripture and then asked him, "Do you want to accept Jesus as your personal Lord and Savior, right now?" He looked me straight in the eye and said, "Yes." He reached out and took my hand and we prayed the sinner's prayer together. He was no longer laughing about Christian Harley people! I then gave him some brief instructions. I also left him with a tract in his hand with the prayer we just prayed and encouraged him to find a good bible-based church. He said he had a Bible at home but hadn't read it. I told him to read the Gospel of John first and go from there. He seemed a little stunned by the incident but was obviously happy and hugged me.

Several minutes later a black man approached us and said he was low on gas and just needed a few bucks to get him home. I was applying suntan lotion at the time. I engaged him in small talk, but he started to walk away seemingly thinking I wouldn't help him. I asked him not to go and told him I would give him some money, but he would have to listen to me talk first, so I could get the lotion off my hands before I reached into my pocket. He agreed.

I then asked him bluntly if He had Jesus in his life and he said yes. I asked if Jesus was his Lord and Savior and again, he said yes. We then talked about his faith and some of his problems. He said he went to a church frequently but didn't read his Bible as often as he should. I gave him some words of encouragement and asked if I could pray for him. He said yes and Sandman and I prayed for him, his family, and his problems. We then shook hands and hugged one another. Sandman and I then each gave him some money. He said we made his day and walked away a happy camper.

When we got to Reno we went to where they were setting up all the vendor booths and displays. I shared with the owner of a motorcycle seat business. His nickname was "Fatty." He seemed to take a liking to me and wanted to show me his bike. We had a nice talk and the door opened for a spiritual comment, which I then made. He said there were ministers in his family who told him unless he went to church and pledged money he was going to hell. He was angry about it and touchy about the subject. He didn't close the door, however, and I was able to ask him what he believed.

He said he believed if you kept the Ten Commandments and were a good person you would be okay with God. By then his son Jake had joined us and was intently listening to what I was saying. He kept his mouth shut but was continually nodding his head in agreement. I told Fatty he was on the right track but with the coming of Jesus, God's covenant with man changed to a new covenant. For one thing, I told him "man" was not capable of keeping all of God's commandments, all the time, because we are all sinners by nature. We needed a Savior, a perfect sacrifice, the Lamb of God, who takes away the sins of the world for all who trust and believe in Him. I quoted John 3:16 and 14:6 and several other verses. I also told him how without faith our good works are like filthy rags to God. He listened very intently.

I felt in my spirit I would be pressuring him too much if I asked him to pray with me, though I badly wanted to. Instead, I remembered Romans 10:9. So, I asked him if He believed what I was saying, and he said yes. I asked if he believed Jesus died for our sins and rose from the dead, and again he said yes. I then asked him, based on this belief, if Jesus was his Lord and Savior and he said, "Yes." He told me he believed in Jesus and he confessed Jesus as his Lord and Savior. Remember the verse, "If you declare with your mouth, 'Jesus is Lord,' and believe in your heart that God raised him from the dead, you will be saved" (Romans 10:9, NIV).

I didn't want to "trample the crops" and left him with a blessing and happy thoughts. I was also able to answer his questions about things he called "sticky points" in his faith.

Fatty left to attend to his customers and Jake stepped forward and told me he was a believer and had been wanting so desperately for his dad to accept Jesus. He had just witnessed him doing so. I told him it was a start in the right direction and to support what we had just done by being a good witness to his dad through his thoughts, words, and behavior. I then asked Jake if I could pray for him and his dad, and he agreed. We prayed together and then shook hands and hugged. He made me promise I would come back, which I did the next day. I gave both Fatty and Jake the little tracts we had made up and even laminated. It was another divine appointment, and the Holy Spirit led the way.

That night, as we returned to our room, we met a plain-clothes security officer in the parking lot. He worked for the Casino where we were staying at the Motor Lodge. I felt prompted to open a spiritual discussion after only a few minutes of small talk. He began telling me of some of the problems he had encountered in his life. I could identify with some of his heartaches and gave him my testimony. We must have talked for forty-five minutes.

I then asked him if he had Jesus in his life and he smiled and pointed to a small crucifix tie tack that he was wearing. He then went into detail about how the Lord had taken everything from him including his wife, family, and possessions. He said he was "brought" to Reno for a reason, but he didn't know what it was. He has been there since shortly after the tragedy of 9-11. The officer said he noticed a "glow" around me when we first met and knew he wanted to talk with me. It was an uplifting and exciting conversation, standing there alone in the dark. Sandman had drifted away to give us privacy when he saw how the conversation was going. The officer and I exchanged hugs and went our separate ways. Another divine appointment? It sure felt like it to me! Sometimes we plant, sometimes we water, and sometimes we harvest. I love it all.

30

Cancer Scourge

Due to my lifelong interest in ballistics, I had started a ballistics consulting business as mentioned in Chapter 5. It was directed toward military special ops and hunters to provide improved accuracy in the field. It was a labor of love, and it helped bring in some extra money. By this time Mom had moved into a retirement community. I had purchased her house and was living alone.

One morning I got a call from my doctor. He had recently taken a biopsy sample from just below my right lower eyelid. He thought it was nothing to worry about at the time and had even made fun of me in front of his nurse for "worrying too much." But he wasn't laughing now. He said it came back positive for melanoma and I needed to get in to see a dermatologist right away.

After getting the call, I let it sink in for a moment, then I got a smile on my face. For some reason, I felt at peace. I shut down my computer, poured a fresh cup of coffee, strolled out onto the back patio, and gazed at the mountains to the west. It was especially stunning. I smelled my coffee and thought how awesome it smelled.

I took a deep breath of the fresh morning air and noticed how crisp it was. Those are just a few of the little things we miss out on as we go about our busy daily lives. But that day, at that moment, I realized how the little things in life can be so special. Yet, when we take them for granted each day, their grandeur seems to slowly diminish until we hardly notice. But at that moment in time, those things came back to me. I felt fantastic! I immediately got excited about how I could use this experience as a witness in my ministry.

After getting the news, I ignored the business for a couple of days and concentrated even more on my ministry. Everyday things just didn't seem so important. Life is fleeting. Maybe my time was coming. Who knows! But I realized I needed to be ready, and I needed to be about the Lord's work. As I thought about it, I decided to start sending out e-mails to catch up with a select group of friends and associates, some saved, some not. I got a great response back and more doors started to open for witnessing and ministry. After the diagnosis, I went to a dermatologist and was immediately scheduled for surgery.

On the day of the procedure, the friendly Italian doctor took good care of me. I had ridden there on my motorcycle which probably wasn't the best decision but the weather was perfect and I love to ride.

The doctor said the cancer was very close to my eye, which is so close to the brain that he wanted to make sure we got it right the first time. The procedure was painless, and I was in and out in about an hour. My right eye was bandaged over as I carefully slipped my helmet on. By the time I hit the freeway I could feel blood running down my cheek. I didn't care, it was over and now I could continue with my life, come what may! Within days I got a call from the doctor. He said when he sent the tissue to the lab, they had not only found melanoma (stage 3) but also basil cell and squamous cell carcinoma in the sample as well. But the good news was that all the borders were clear. During my follow-up with the doctor, I asked him what was next, and he confidently said with a laugh, "Go home, you're healed!" He then recommended I have complete skin exams biannually.

I had to think, what if I hadn't pressed the first doctor to remove that spot? He had even made fun of me about it being nothing. But something had told me not to listen to him and to *insist* it be removed. As it turned out it was already at stage 3. At stage 4 the melanoma cells shotgun to your lungs, liver, brain, digestive system, and lymph nodes.

The whole ordeal impressed upon me how the Lord had plans for my life and my time wasn't up yet. It also showed me how much my heart was truly consumed with ministry and sharing my faith. Have you ever heard the saying, "Never let a good crisis go to waste," by Winston Churchill? I think there is a good lesson in that. First of all, what can we learn from our crisis? And second, how can we use it to our advantage?

What I learned was that I had nothing to fear and that Jesus had my six! I knew I would not pass from this life one second before God was ready to summon me home. That time is an unknown. So, what do we do? Like the Apostle Paul, we press on. When I put things in that perspective the answer came naturally. We are here to serve God, love one another, and to glorify Him. We shouldn't just keep our faith to ourselves, we should share it with others. Also, the Bible says, "Be wise as serpents and harmless a doves" (Mat 10:16 KJV). It didn't take me long to discover how to use the cancer threat to encourage others to seek the Lord and to have no fear, and that's exactly what I did.

Through the ordeal, I found when I would casually mention my diagnosis to a non-believer, their first reaction was one of shock and fear. They would often say, "Aren't you scared, you seem so nonchalant?" That would be my opening to gently witness to them. It would be my opportunity to tell them the reason for the joy that was in my heart (1 Pet 3:15). And when doing so, I never felt even a hint of rejection. I could clearly see how God can cause all things to work together for good, for those who love Him and are called according to His purpose (paraphrased, Rom 8:28). I had used "the scourge" as a witnessing tool by exhibiting joy, peace, and a faith which had set me free.

31

"O Death Where is Thy Sting?"

AH, BUT THE Devil wasn't through sifting me. About a year later, during a routine medical exam, my doctor (a new one) noticed I had a small lump in my throat and felt I should see a specialist, which of course I did. They tried to probe the area and snip a little sample for the lab. But as they tried, I kept getting so nauseated that they decided to stop and do exploratory surgery under sedation on another day.

When the time rolled around, before going in for the follow-up surgery, my club brothers wanted to pray over me. The doctor was there at the time and asked if he could stay with us while they prayed, which was pretty cool. I could feel their positive energy and just knew everything was going to be fine.

After the surgery, the doctor said where he expected to find cancer there was none. But he had noticed several other nodules in another spot that looked very suspicious. So, he decided to remove them along with half the thyroid gland. He sent the tissue to the lab as per medical protocol. It turned out one of the samples was cancerous, however, it was all contained in the sample. Afterward, he said he felt confident there was no need to go back in to remove the rest of my thyroid but rather monitor it with ultrasound semi-annually for a while. I was good with this because I believed in my heart I had been delivered from the insidious curse.

"O Death Where is Thy Sting?"

I slept at the hospital overnight and was released the next day. There had been tremendous support from my ministry friends who sat with my family until I was stabilized. Sandman had even come from Fresno to stay with me. What a blessing they all were.

A short time after the thyroid surgery, I began to realize how much my back was hurting. Before long I could hardly walk. I began taking the Vicodin the surgeon had prescribed for post-surgery throat pain to medicate myself for the back pain, which was much worse. I'd had a bad back for twenty-five years, but it had mostly been in manageable episodes lasting only a few days or so. But this went on and on and kept getting worse. I had done nothing new to aggravate my back that I could think of.

I began to blame it on Satan and thought since he couldn't stop my witnessing by cursing me with cancer, he was now attacking me in another way. But I began witnessing even more. Just before my thyroid surgery, I had given my testimony at two churches on the same day.

I ran through my short supply of Vicodin and just tried to ignore the pain. Then we took another ministry trip down to SoCal, riding our Harleys several hundred miles to get there again. Upon arrival, I could hardly walk more than ten feet at a time, but I was determined to crusade for the Lord and be there for my brothers. Chapo was going to be formally ordained and I wanted to support him. Finally, someone offered me half of a pain pill (Norco) that was like Vicodin, but stronger. I reluctantly took half of one in desperation and the pain subsided to a more manageable level. Then I took the other half that night to help get me through.

When I got back home, I began trying to get in to see an orthopedic surgeon. Meanwhile, I had to deal with the pain. Thankfully, I was able to get in to see my regular doctor, and he in turn recommended I see a pain management specialist until I could see an orthopedist. When I saw the pain doc, I told him I had previously taken Norco for pain and how it had given me some relief. So, that is what he prescribed, along with Vioxx to reduce the swelling around the spine until I could get an appointment with the orthopedist.

Shortly afterward I was armed with a two-week supply of Norco and Vioxx. I hated taking the stuff because I didn't want to become addicted. I no longer used alcohol, and rarely took even Tylenol. I proceeded to go without any medication to get through my home-based workday, and then around four o'clock in the afternoon, I would desperately need some relief. It started with only half a pill, then a whole one, then one-and-a-half, then two, then eventually up to three within several hours! Whatever it took to put a dent in the relentless pain, I would do. Then, when I felt some relief from the medication, I would try to get a few more things done, usually staying up until 1:00 AM.

After that, I couldn't get to sleep and would toss and turn in pain all night long. Instead of a sedation effect, for some reason, the meds kept me awake. Then the next day I would feel wasted. This went on for weeks. Meanwhile, I had gotten back to see the pain doc again and got a new prescription for Norco as well as something to help me sleep. At times I had to take a double dose of my sleeping medication just to get some rest. I would toss and turn until about 3:00 AM and then crash until about 10 AM, sometimes noon!

That was depressing to me because I had always been accustomed to getting up with the sun and feeling great. While all this was going on, I was keeping up my ballistics consulting and ministry networking. The ministry kept me on a fiery roll (at least spiritually). Like everything in life I had ever done, I jumped in with both feet and was going for the gusto. I was burning the candle at both ends, working, ministering, and witnessing for the Lord. But I was slowly becoming more depressed as the pain was taking its toll. Then of course I began feeling guilty about all the drugs. I couldn't stand the pain and I still wasn't cleared by my worker's comp insurance to see an orthopedic surgeon.

It became a vicious cycle. Around four o'clock in the afternoon, as the pain would increase, I would become nauseated and start to get cramps in my stomach. I would also get hot flashes, sweats, and more depressing thoughts. It was horrible and I became disgusted with my situation. I had become physically and mentally dependent on the painkillers. I wasn't suicidal, but I prayed the Lord would just take me home so the suffering would end. I soon got to where I couldn't stand to look at myself in the mirror.

For one thing, I had become deeply embedded in the motorcycle club culture. I felt it would be an asset (like the Apostle Paul) to, "... become all things to all men, so that I might by all means save some" (1 Corinthians 9:22, NKJV). Our ministry focuses on the hardcore outlaw motorcycle club types. My head was shaved and my beard was down to my chest. It had been growing for thirteen months. I had also accumulated a wild assortment of tattoos, all ministry related. I guess I looked like a wild man with my black leathers and Black & White club patch, rolling down the highway with my beard blowing in the wind. It was fun and the culture itself can be very alluring, but depression from the pain and the meds were putting me in a bad place.

One secular biker motto is "Ride to Live, Live to Ride." The Harley, the culture, and even the ministry can become an idol if we're not careful. It's supposed to be about Jesus and servitude, right? "He must increase, but I must decrease" (John 3:30, NKJV). I was continually checking myself, knowing all too well the weakness of the flesh. And, of course, Satan is always lurking in the shadows somewhere, lying, tempting, and challenging us to look at things his way. It is forever his joy to accuse us before the Lord.

I continued to read my Bible, twice a day for hours, even when I was soaking my back. I prayed relentlessly, although I was almost too depressed at times to even try. Despite the pain, I knew I had to get off the meds, so one day I just quit. Then nausea, stomach cramping, back and neck pain, and depression came on like gangbusters. I was miserable. As I would read the Bible, Satan would put doubt and *confusion* in my mind, but alas, our "God is not a god of confusion, but of peace, as in all the churches of the saints..." (1 Corinthians 14:33, NASB).

I would sometimes find a *perceived* contradiction in the Bible. Then I would again pray and go to the commentaries in my library, and the internet, to search for the truth and any enlightenment I could find. But I wanted to withdraw from people. I literally couldn't call anyone. I just couldn't deal with it. Yet when someone called me or when I went out, I would often pretend everything was okay. I had become clinically depressed.

One day I came home and was so overcome with pain and depression I dropped to my knees in the kitchen. I was broken. My home felt like a dungeon. It was like God had been ripped out of my chest. He was gone, or so it seemed. Then I heard a voice in my head say, "Where's your God now?" I felt it was Satan trying to pull me down even lower. He was laughing at me. I yelled at him, "Get out of my house, get away from me ... I will never turn my back on Jesus!" I told Satan the Holy Spirit dwelled in me and I had complete power over him. I repeated, "Get out in the name of Jesus!"

Sins which were long ago confessed in prayer and repented of, which had already been washed away by the blood of Jesus, came flashing back to me in vivid detail. That's how the devil works. He wants to rub our noses in our messes and accuse us before God. I remembered people I had let down, and times of selfishness, pride, and vanity. I saw snippets of faces, words, and emotional pain I had inflicted on others. I felt worthless and desolate. I was struck with the realization of how people in our lives come and go, and even die. Nothing lasts! Material "treasures" break, wear out, burn up, and return to dust. Pleasures are fleeting and temporary. I began thinking the only thing that really matters is our relationship with God and our loved ones, helping others, and sharing the Gospel with the lost as best we can. But in the moment, I felt so alone and helpless. I was still living alone as Reann and I weren't married yet. But as hard as she tried to help and comfort me, the pain and the depression, as well as feeling devoid of God, had me trapped in a very dark place.

I had recently seen Mel Gibson's movie, *The Passion of the Christ*, and I flashed back to the crucifixion. I thought of Jesus's burden of taking the sins of the whole world upon Himself (1 John 2:2, KJV) and becoming sin for us (2 Corinthians 5:21, NKJV) as the flawless sacrifice for our sins, while at the same time feeling abandoned by His Father. Life had become unbearable for me, yet I knew my situation paled in comparison to what Jesus suffered.

Satan kept trying to pull me farther down. If I thought about my ministry, the brothers I ride with, and even my motorcycle, I would become nauseated and flushed and would start sweating. I couldn't even stand to look at the patch on my leather cut. It was unreal. I began to grope for the meaning of it all. I still didn't know for sure what was happening, but I had a strong feeling God was going to pull me out of it.

Then, out of the blue, I got a phone call from Jimmy Moss. Jimmy had been a ministry member previously. He was an ex-con who had spent much of his adult life in prison. I shared with Jimmy what I was going through. I also told him I had stopped taking my pain meds. He said to me, "Bro, you're detoxing." He said I had all the classic symptoms. He also said this happened for a reason and

God was going to use this incident in my life as a powerful witness. He was extremely compassionate and reassuring. He told me about all the pain he had gone through while in prison and on the streets, and each time he had gone through heroin withdrawals.

I knew I was on the right track after Jimmy's call. God doesn't waste pain and suffering. There are lessons to be learned. Surprisingly, his call was followed by a call from my chiropractor's office saying that the orthopedist's office had been trying repeatedly to call me to get me in. But because of privacy statutes, they couldn't leave a message because my answering machine indicated they had reached a business and not a residence.

I immediately called the orthopedist's office, and the receptionist was completely astonished when she found there was an opening in two days. She even said, "This can't be right, somebody must have made a mistake. This doctor is always booked solid!" After checking it out she said there had just been a cancellation freeing up an eight AM spot. I jumped on it!

That night I got a call from Sandman in Fresno. Him being a nurse practitioner, he was able to confirm everything Jimmy had said. He also told me to get back on the Vioxx I had been taking because it was non-addictive and would reduce the swelling around my spine. He said he felt I was still in so much pain because the dosage of Vioxx I had been taking was too low. He said I should double it. His call turned out to be a blessing because I followed his advice and doubled up on the Vioxx and by the next morning I felt some improvement. Two days later, I went to the orthopedist's appointment. The doctor confirmed Sandman's recommendation was correct. I still had to contend with the pain, withdrawal symptoms, and severe depression, but I could finally see some light at the end of the tunnel and that gave me hope.

"O Death Where is Thy Sting?"

Due to serious side effects in some patients, Vioxx has since been taken off the market. However, my experience with it was good, and it helped get me through at the time. I am not here to give medical advice, nor am I qualified, so if you have any drugs laying around the house, please always consult your doctor first.

While going through this, I still wanted to witness to as many people as I could. Although my attempts were feeble at best, I wanted God to know I still trusted and believed in Him and would wait on Him to tell me what to do. I was still going through the medical issues, but I was getting re-energized and feeling a little better each day. I was also prescribed an anti-depression med, which started kicking in within a week. Wow, what a relief.

I had already been through back injections previously and they did no good whatsoever. But now it was finally approved to take things to the next level. The back doctor requested an MRI and the results showed I needed surgery to trim a disk between L4 and L5. It was bulging and pushing into the spinal nerve. He said he could see the problem clearly and wanted to get me in as soon as possible. Within a week I was on the table, prepped for surgery, and good to go. Finally!

Afterward, when I came out of anesthesia, the surgeon dropped by and asked how the pain was. It was gone! I finally had relief. It took a little while to get my legs back under me, but the fix had worked. I was finally on the mend. I was told it is very common to go into a deep depression after long periods of intense pain and that my meds were now nicely balanced and on course. Thank the Lord for doctors!

I reflected on the time when Jesus said to Simon Peter, "Simon, Simon, behold, Satan has demanded permission to sift you like wheat" (Luke 22:31, NASB). We should check our pride daily to keep ourselves in the right frame of mind. When tempted to sin we should ask ourselves, "Is this thought coming from God or from the devil?" I repeatedly work at keeping my life and ministry in perspective. Even more so after this experience. A lot of the hits we take in our lives are coming from the enemy, so we must always be aware and vigilant! If we understand our enemy, we will be better and wiser warriors.

Satan didn't get to win this battle, but it was one heck of a fight, not to mention multi-dimensional. I was learning to adapt to situations, examine myself, and stay committed. God had a plan in all this. For one thing, I was thoroughly humbled before the Lord. Without Him I was powerless. Through this process, I was shown what it is like to have "Christ in me" and what it was like to have Him "missing in action." He was never gone, it was just a work being completed in me. I had been pruned, and Satan had ridiculed and tested me as well. I was being strengthened and hardened for battles yet to come. I'm on a long spiritual journey and the learning will not end until the Lord calls me home.

Recently, to stay tuned in, I started reading spiritually informative books, written by top biblical scholars. I also felt if I could increase my reading speed, I could learn more at a faster rate. I enrolled in a speed-reading course online. I also began re-reading the whole Bible once again, cover to cover.

After the speed-reading course, I started going through a lot of books. While digging through my home library, I found an old book by Charles H. Spurgeon, *The Soul Winner: How to Lead Sinners to the Savior*.

As I was reading it, I was deeply drawn into his world. He had a burning passion for teaching the Word and winning souls. There is no greater endeavor than serving God, praising His holy name, giving Him the glory for all things good, loving our neighbors as ourselves, and leading others to a glorious personal relationship with Jesus the Christ.

If anyone involved in evangelistic ministry is going through suppression of the Spirit, the pain of pruning, and finding no explanation for the cause, there is a chapter in Mr. Spurgeon's book called *"The Cost of Being a Soul Winner."* It is a must-read chapter. How many of us have experienced the peaks and valleys, the ebbs and flows of our spiritual journeys? You might just find some encouraging answers in his book.

As I read through the chapter, it reminded me of some of my own experiences. I was becoming enlightened, and my spirit was being satisfied. It led me to pray, "If I need to be pruned, then prune me, Lord! If I need to be toughened, then toughen me, Lord! And if I need to be disciplined, then discipline me, Lord." If we humble ourselves before the Lord, we will always emerge stronger, wiser, and more effective. "God resists the proud but gives grace to the humble" (1 Peter 5:6, NKJV).

As I worked through Spurgeon's book, every chapter had solid food of great value for every believer. And now, as I continue to build my spiritual physique, I can clearly see the truth in the phrases *no pain, no gain* and *never give up!*

32

AN EXTRA REP FOR JESUS!

ONE DAY WHILE working out at the gym, I ran into a biker who I'd seen in various gyms and at rallies over the years. He rode a black Harley Road Glide. He's a big boy, his name is Roy, and he stands about six-foot-four and weighed probably 240 pounds. He was in his late forties at the time and was a Vietnam war vet. He said hi and struck up a conversation. He talked about his investments and the women in his life. He also mentioned going to a singles bar and seeking "something new." He said I should try it. I told him there wasn't anything there I needed. He looked at me like I was out of my mind and said, "Where do you go? How do you get it?"

I told him, "I don't" (this was still before Reann and I had gotten married). He walked away shaking his head in wonderment. I immediately said a silent prayer for him: "Lord, have mercy on that poor lost soul. How could anyone like me get through to him? Lord, have mercy on him." I felt compassion and despair. I felt so inadequate! No sooner had I said "Amen" to my prayer than he turned around and walked back to me and started asking questions about my life. He said he had always felt I had a peace about me and wanted to know where I found it.

When I told him I was a Christian he chuckled saying, "So, what does that have to do with anything?" I told him it had everything to do with *everything* and how I gave my life to Jesus and simply try to follow the teachings of the Bible. He walked away again, but again he came back. He wanted to know more. So, I told him Jesus was the answer and all I needed. I further told him Jesus provided me with a peace I couldn't find in alcohol, sex, rock-n-roll, hot Harleys, or the fast life. I told him I wasn't afraid to die anymore and, as for sex, I abstained, in an attempt to be obedient to the Scriptures. Then I laughed and said, "I guess I must sound like a nut case to you huh?"

He looked at me seriously and said, "No, not really, I respect you for that." He again walked away, only to return once more. He told me he didn't have peace inside and desperately needed it.

I told him there was only one way to get it. The Holy Spirit then gave me verse after verse to share with him. I asked if he would like to discuss it some more after his workout. He said he would. About ten minutes later he walked over and asked me when I was leaving. I smiled and said I was only waiting on him (I might add neither of us was finished with our workout). As we walked out of the gym, I prayed silently in my mind to not get ahead of the Lord and asked the Holy Spirit to guide me according to His divine will.

To get out of the night air we took a seat in my Jeep. I told him all about Jesus and asked him if he believed what I was telling him. He said he did. He then told me about lives taken in Vietnam and things that troubled him. He asked me if he could be forgiven. I quoted and paraphrased more scripture. We then further discussed forgiveness as well as women and fornication. Again, I told him what the Bible says. He sat deep in thought. I told him that where his treasures were, there his heart would be also (Matthew 6:21). I told him Jesus wanted his heart and the Lord had brought us together for me to point him toward the Light. Deep in thought, he nodded quietly.

I asked him if he understood and believed all I had shared with him, and he said he did. I reached into the back seat and retrieved a brand-new copy of a Biker Bible we use in our ministry. I handed it to him and told him to read the Gospel of John first. He asked me to earmark it for him. I then asked him if he wanted to have the peace of Jesus I had found and to ask Jesus into his heart as his personal Lord and Savior, and once again he said yes.

I told him I didn't want him to be influenced by the power of persuasiveness but by the power of the spirit within him. It had to come from his heart. I asked if it was in his heart to surrender his life to the Lord and he said, "Yes, I need peace." Roy took my hand in a biker grip and prayed the sinner's prayer with me, giving his heart to the Lord. I wrote my name and phone number in the Bible, as well as the date, telling him it was the date of his spiritual birth and how his eternity with Jesus began the moment he first believed and confessed Jesus as Lord.

This was one of the most powerful salvations I've had the honor to facilitate. He was a hardcore case as a secular biker and Vietnam vet, and a person filled with lust for the things of this world and guilt for the lives taken in war. One minute he was reveling in the things of the world and wondering what being a Christian had to do with anything, and thirty minutes later he accepted Jesus Christ as his personal Lord and Savior.

As I drove home, I prayed to God, thanking Him for letting me see yet another miracle. It was too incredible to believe, had I not seen it so many times before. God laid it on my heart right then: "Foolish one! You were thinking in terms of the flesh, not the Spirit. With *Me* all things are possible!" On the way home I prayed out loud and teared up, thanking God for His goodness and mercy. I will never forget it! God hears our prayers and answers them in His time and His way. As His servants He simply wants us to follow Him and to step out in faith. He is in control. Praise His Holy Name!

33

WHERE CHAPO FOUND GOD

I MET UP with Brother Chapo at Starbucks for coffee one day, and he related the following story to me:

Chapo was saved while doing time in prison. He had been placed in solitary confinement due to his violent tendencies. He said he was possessed by a demon and had been violent and combative for years. In his emptiness and pain, he cried out to the Lord and asked Him to reveal Himself. He said, "Lord if you're real, I need to know!" He said he heard God say, "I am real!" He said it was as real as if the Lord were right there with him in the hole. He said, "I knew it was God." Chapo had been a high-level gangster. He had been an addict, a drug dealer, an armed robber, and a killer. He had also been a minion of Satan and had performed satanic rituals.

Right after Chapo's God experience, he was unexpectedly returned to his normal cell and decided to talk to a couple of his cellmates who he knew were Christians. He asked them if they would think he was crazy if he told them God had just spoken to him. They said, "No Brother, not at all!" He then told them if God was real then he wanted to know Him.

As they explained the Gospel message to Chapo and prayed with him, he blanked out. When he came to, he said he was black and blue and all beat up from being bounced off the bars, metal bunks, and the cell walls. His cellies believed he had been possessed by demons and they were purged out of him when he gave his heart to the Lord and confessed Jesus as his Lord and Savior. Things immediately began to change in Chapo. He had a newfound peace about him. Later that day, there was a chapel call and Brother Chapo raised his hand and asked to attend.

Chapo was in prison for attempted homicide of a peace officer. He had committed an armed robbery and as he sped off in his getaway vehicle, a deputy sheriff jumped in front of him, but Chapo kept it floored, grazing the deputy and causing bodily harm. Chapo was subsequently arrested, convicted, and sentenced to serve his time at Chino State Prison.

When Chapo got out (much earlier than he expected), he found a good church and attended regularly, working at rounding off all his rough edges. He also started sharing his faith with others, including his dad. His dad, Bob, was a gangster type too and ran with a rough crowd. He wanted nothing to do with Chapo's newfound faith.

Chapo began praying regularly for his dad (who had given him his nickname which means "Shorty" in Spanish, which is funny because Chapo was six feet tall). During one of his prayer sessions, God again spoke to Chapo, assuring him nothing would happen to his dad without him being saved first by God's grace. Then one day Chapo got a call saying his dad had been shot and to come to the hospital immediately. Upon his arrival, Chapo found out his dad had been shot in the body and the head and how he had lain at the crime scene for over four hours, bleeding out. He was declared dead at the scene, as well as "dead on arrival" at the hospital.

Chapo was led to a small room where his dad's body lay on a gurney in the dark. He was completely covered with a sheet. Chapo was devastated and began crying out to the Lord. He told the Lord He had promised nothing bad would happen to his dad unless he was saved first. He angrily told God he was holding Him to that

Where Chapo Found God

promise. As Chapo wept over his dad, he heard a faint sound, like someone struggling to breathe. As he looked closer, he could see the sheet puffing up around his dad's face. He then apprehensively pulled back the sheet and saw that his dad's eyes were blinking, and he was trying to breathe!

Chapo quickly ran into the hallway and yelled for help. But the staff calmly assured him his dad had been dead on arrival. Chapo yelled back that if his dad was dead, then why was he struggling to breathe and blinking his eyes? Aid came quickly and Chapo's dad was immediately revived and given a blood transfusion. Bob survived his dance with death and began his recovery.

He was paralyzed from the neck down because of the gunshot wounds. Chapo took his dad into his home and cared for him daily. One day he told Chapo to "Go get Pastor Dick, I need to know more about Jesus." Chapo's dad was led to the Lord that very day and God's promise was fulfilled. Chapo had to bathe, dress, shave, and feed his dad. One day he said, "Chapo, I wasn't a good dad to you, why are you so good to me?" Chapo responded, "Because you're my dad and I love you."

Bob was confined to a wheelchair at first but then started getting feelings in his hands and legs. He went from the wheelchair to a walker, to crutches, and then to a cane. Before long he was leaving his cane in a corner and walking on his own. A good number of years later, Bob Garcia passed away of natural causes, after spending some good years with his family, his son Chapo, and his daughter-in-law Katherine. I went to the memorial service over which Pastor Dick presided. He explained the gospel's message of salvation at the end and six of Chapo's family members went forward to give their hearts to Jesus. A normally sad and solemn event filled with grief turned into an incredibly happy celebration as spirits rejoiced and united. It was awesome to behold!

34

HERE WE GO AGAIN!

NOT AGAIN! BY now, I should know to thank God for the bad as well as the good He allows us to experience. He calls the shots and in the end uses all things for the good! But the valleys are so painful. Why so soon Lord? The last episode was only about four months back! I felt as if God had somehow withdrawn from me again. When I called out to God, all I heard back was an echo in my soul. I would walk around the house, saying out loud, "Lord, hello, Lou here. Are you there? I'm still here!" You would think I would have learned by now! Why are we such knuckleheads?

In my spirit I remembered, "Be still, and know that I am God" (Psalm 46:10, NIV). For one thing, I needed to learn to be more patient. It's not about my will and timing, but God's. During this time Satan tempted me to just give up. He gently manipulated my mind, trying to justify evil thoughts of everything we are taught to resist. He tried to convince me I had gone too far with Jesus and should find a more *worldly* balance. But I continued to pray and give everything up to the Lord. I told Him my resolve was to stand firm. And to Satan I said, "Get out!"

I felt perhaps the motorcycle ministry was starting to slip away. So I said, "Okay Lord, whatever you want. I will be still and know that you are God and that you are in control." So I prayed and stayed in the Word, reading the Bible daily.

Here we go again!

I kept going about my daily routine and trusting in the Lord. By now my back was greatly improved. That helped for sure. I was even able to resume my gym workouts and I began eating more healthy foods. My physical, mental, and spiritual health all began to improve. I've always had my ups and downs, and a few setbacks, but I've kept looking up, trying to always keep my focus on the Cross. What else was I to learn from this latest episode? Perhaps Satan was simply trying to steal my joy.

I was astounded the Lord was using a sinner like me as a messenger. I was being asked to speak publicly more and more often. I previously had a fear of public speaking and still do, I guess. But I just couldn't refuse an opportunity to serve the Lord. I found if I stepped forward in faith, He would take charge and get me through or over any obstacles. Blind faith and a willingness to obey were all that was required. It reminded me of so many parts of the Bible where simple faith solved all the problems.

I started praying for the Lord to keep me humble and to strip me of any self-pride and ego involvement. As I read the Bible, God continued to speak to me through His Word, *"Be still—listen, listen—this is the day the Lord has made, rejoice and be glad in it—be still and know that I am God—I am in control—I must increase, but you must decrease—be still."*

As I pondered this revelation, I realized how true it was. Could it be I had lost touch with *who* is really in control? I had volunteered from the beginning to fight on the front lines of spiritual warfare. I wanted to get my licks in. Don't hold me down, don't hold me back, I want to fight to the death! Well, perhaps I was simply getting what I asked for!

But God made it very clear, He didn't *need* me, He doesn't need anybody! He loves me and He simply wants me to *remember my place* and to be obedient to Him. Remember when God told

Moses in the desert to "speak to the rock" and it would bring forth water for the people? Instead, Moses got irritated and angry at the people who were turning away from God, and he *struck* the rock with his staff two times. He took over and did it *his* way, not the way God had directed. That cost him a trip across the Jordan River to the Promised Land. God was giving me some direction here and I needed to pay attention.

I felt a stirring in my spirit and I began to pray, "Okay Lord, teach me to be still. Teach me to *listen*." As I prayed, He seemed to put the word "listen" in my head more and more. I have never been a good listener. I was always too wrapped up in myself and trying to teach others. But how do we know what or how to teach if we don't listen as well? I asked God to help me grow in this area, "Lord, help me to be still, help me to be a better listener."

I began riding my Harley a little more and again was blessed by the warm breeze on my face. I began to ride just to enjoy the ride. Daily I began to feel more refreshed. I was afraid to take anything for granted and began to praise the Lord for every battle won against temptation, for the beauty of the day, for the sights, sounds, and smells of all His creation. And for all my blessings as well. My peace with the Lord was slowly being restored. There is no doubt many things had happened to me, all at the same time. Then, while I was at my weakest, I was again attacked by the enemy. He always loves to kick us when we're down.

I continued going to services at the Atascadero Bible Church (ABC). At the time, they were promoting a group study about our purpose here on Earth and what God expects from us. Pastor Tom had asked for people to volunteer their homes to host classes about the topic. All the study materials were nicely printed out into study handbooks as were curriculum guidelines for the leaders. The classes were to run for six weeks, with a class once a week.

Here we go again!

I just didn't know if I could commit. I was still staying pretty much to myself, living alone, praying, reading the Word, licking my wounds, and indulging in a little self-pity. I didn't think I was up to being a host and opening up my home. I procrastinated until the last minute. The church was having a prayer time for us to pray for an anointing for the upcoming classes, which were about to begin. I found myself there at ABC, praying along with everyone. I knew I needed to participate somehow in the classes, so afterward I approached Pastor Ron Smith. He told me I was too late as all the classes were already full. I realized this could get my conscience off the hook but instead, I said in a joking manner, "Well, I'll just have to do my own class then!"

Pastor Ron looked up with a big grin and said, "Would you like to?" It then came to me that our motorcycle ministry could greatly benefit from this class, as could I. When I told him so, he thought it was a great idea and he hooked me up with other associates who provided me with the workbooks and other materials.

When I got home, I called Chapo and ran the idea by him. He said he would talk with Pastor Clayton at the First Assembly of God church in Templeton to see if we could use a meeting room there. The ball was rolling, and we got a thumbs up from the pastor.

The same day my class was to begin, I ran into Pastor Tom. I asked him for a copy of his introductory sermon about the topic I would be teaching, and he was happy to share it with me. When I went home to prepare for the first class that night, I first read the introduction from the workbook I was supposed to present to the class. Then I grabbed the notes from Tom. They were the perfect lead-in for the first class! No one in the class I was about to teach attended the ABC church, so none of them had heard it before. It was perfect!

As I've said, I normally don't like to speak in public (I'm more of a one-on-one street evangelist), but the Lord seemed to be putting this on my heart and I wanted to be obedient. Besides, I already knew all the people who would be there. I gave it up to Him and asked for His blessing and anointing. I could feel the excitement building in my spirit as I realized God was calling me forward again.

The class went great that night and we had a new decision for Jesus! Remember Roy, the guy from the gym? It was his daughter Karlisha. Roy was there as well. There were also several rededications that evening. What a blessing it was! I was thrilled beyond words. We went on to finish the series without a hitch.

Soon afterward Mother's Day rolled around and I took my mom to church at ABC. After returning home, I changed clothes and was going to catch a little wind on my bike. As I was about to leave, I got a call. It was Pastor Clayton from Chapo's church. He said he was in a real bind and had to leave town. He said he needed someone to preach the 6:00 PM sermon and his backup pastor was sick. I was caught completely off-guard and must admit I felt a little speechless. "You mean you want *me* to preach the sermon?" I asked.

"Yeah, that's right," he responded. He said he knew I dearly loved the Lord, and the Lord would help me through it if I would agree. I stumbled over my words for a few moments as I realized my commitment to the Lord. He also threw in how Pastor Chapo had recommended me. Then I knew I had to do it. I told Pastor Clayton I happened to have a sermon I could modify for the service. He thanked me and hung up.

Now there I was, standing with the phone in my hand thinking; "Lord, how in the world did this happen? Just a couple of weeks ago I was crying out for you to re-fill me with the Holy Spirit, to not leave me as an orphan, but to use me again. I had felt so empty, and now look what has happened! Do you trust me this much?" I then said,

Here we go again!

"Yes Lord, I will do this for you because your hand is on it. I ask for your blessing and anointing, in Jesus's name. Amen."

That afternoon I picked my mom up and took her with me to Pastor Clayton's church. In obedience to the Lord, I preached Pastor Tom's sermon (what would I have done without it?). I was humbled. Praise God! Thank you, Jesus! What's next I thought?

35

Fair Game

At the time the Last Disciples were having our weekly meetings at a local Starbucks. I got there first, as usual. As I waited out front, two guys in their early thirties approached me. They said they rode with the 81 down south and were not members but had been born into the R&W family. They said their dads, uncles, and cousins were all involved. One of them said his name was Sam and the other was a lanky kid named Jason. Jason asked to see my back patch. They were complimentary when I turned around and showed it to them. Then Sam blurted out he was raised in a Christian home. That was a door opener for me, but I didn't push it. I reached into my pocket and handed them each a tract. Jason put his in a pocket, but Sam looked at both sides of his before thanking me and tucking it away. We then parted company.

After my club brothers arrived, we got our coffee and sat out front enjoying the sun. Then Sam and Jason walked by again and I introduced them to the guys. They said about 800 R&Ws were going on a funeral run to San Francisco that afternoon and they would be coming through town. They invited us to ride with them. We politely declined and they went on their way. They just didn't quite seem like the real deal. But what the heck, even wannabes need to be saved. Everyone is fair game, right?

A week later, I was getting off my bike in front of Gary Bang's Harley dealership in Atascadero when I heard someone say, "Hey,

Lou." I turned around and it was Jason and Sam again. Sam came up to me and said he just wanted me to know he had given his heart back to the Lord. I was floored! I said, "Praise God! What did it brother, was it the little tract I gave you?" He said, "Yeah, I read it and decided I wanted to follow Jesus." He said he was leaving his club affiliation behind because he was tired of it all. He said He and Jason were staying at the homeless shelter for the time being. I told Sam he had made my day and he said, "No brother, you made mine." He also said he had been sober for a week (since I had given him the tract) and explained how he tried to drink a beer later in the week and it made him sick to his stomach. Is God awesome or what?

I dug out my last Biker Bible and went to the shelter the next day looking for them, but they weren't around. I think I will be spending more time around the homeless shelter for a while.

When God withdraws, there's always a reason, and we will always emerge stronger. There are always lessons to be learned.

36

WILFREDO

ONE DAY WE got a call from a rehabilitation facility we sometimes refer people to. They asked if we could send someone over to the facility near Fresno, to pick up a guy who was injured in their work recovery program. His name was Wilfredo. Chapo and I had just dropped him off there twelve days prior. Wilfredo was a recovering heroin addict who sincerely wanted to turn his life around. During the ride over there, we discussed the Bible and asked him if he had read any of it. He said he hadn't and had never learned to read or write.

After we arrived to pick him up, he told us how several days after he first got there, he gave his heart to the Lord and became a believer. On the ride back to his home in Oceano, over on the coast, he showed signs of deeply rooted faith and a desire to follow Jesus. He spoke of problems in the facility he wanted to address with the "love of God" upon his return there. It was a blessing to hear him talk!

When we stopped for gas, I told him the Bible would feed him so many truths that would help him to grow in his faith and to move him forward. Then I remembered he couldn't read as I noticed he had a Bible on his lap. I said, "Oh man, I forgot, you can't read, maybe someone at the facility can teach you when you go back."

Wilfredo got this big grin on his face and said, "Watch this, Bro." He opened the Bible and started reading a passage to me. I was blown away! I asked him how he was able to do it and he said he didn't know. He said an old Mexican guy had been working with him and it just started happening. He said the guy had shown him Bible verses in Spanish and English for comparison, but he had never learned to read in Spanish either. In fact, he had never been to school in his entire life! Wilfredo was an immigrant from Puerto Rico.

I asked if anyone had taught him the alphabet yet and he said no. It had only been about ten days since he had given his heart to the Lord, and he was reading! As he read to me, I realized he wasn't reading the words as if he had them memorized, but he read to me as a young child would read. I was astonished. I felt I had witnessed another one of those miracles that seem so easy for us to dismiss as an unusual or strange circumstance. I was blown away by this incident. I think God has some serious plans for Wilfredo!

The above story sounds rather amazing, doesn't it? Do you think things like this happen? Does God perform miracles today as we read of in the Bible? If in doubt, just read this testimony about a pastor's father in Zimbabwe. I found it in a Christian motorcyclist periodical that had been published years ago.

> "His father was an uneducated man who had never attended school and could not read or write. He had accepted Christ as his Savior and came out of a demonic worship atmosphere. He knew that he could not be an effective Christian without being able to read the Bible. He believed God could supernaturally teach him to read. With this faith, he went to the bush—a remote section of Africa—and began to pray. He prayed all day the first day, but nothing happened. He prayed all day the second day with the same results. On the

third day, God spoke to him and said, "You can now read." He had been impressed to start reading 1 Timothy 3. He knew a person who had a Bible and asked him if Timothy was a book in the Bible. The man replied, "Yes," and opened his Bible to 1 Timothy 3 and handed it to the man. He could instantly read God's Word. What a miraculous thing God had done!

This man went on to father four churches before God called him home. What would God do if we would isolate ourselves for three days in prayer, believing Him to do the impossible? Is there anything that God would hold from us to reach the lost? I think not. He sent Jesus to die on a cross so that the world may be saved."

Well, believe what you will. I'm just reporting the accounts as I get them. Amazing Grace!

37

Terri's Fundraiser

ONE DAY WE rode to a fundraiser in Grover Beach, CA, to support Bernard and his wife Terri. The purpose was to raise funds for Terri's medical expenses after their near-fatal motorcycle accident in Reno, Nevada. Terri was still in a Reno hospital at the time, due to her debilitating injuries, and Bernard had to return home without her until she was stabilized. The fundraiser was being hosted by a local White & Gold MC, of which Bernard was the founder and president. About 350 bikers showed up from all around the central California coastal area. In addition to us and the W&G, there were also some R&W, the B&G, and lots of independent bikers (those unaffiliated with any clubs).

It was a social event complete with live music, raffles, and a barbecue. All went smoothly, and everyone had a great time. One of the raffle drawings was called a "Fifty-Fifty," where the winner gets half the overall ticket sales of the raffle, and the other half goes to the fundraiser. The cash prize was $157.

When the winning number was called, the winner was no longer present. So, I was asked by one of the women who was handling all the money to hold the cash until the winner could be called on his cell phone to return and claim it. Pretty soon he showed up and happily claimed his prize. I told him I was an officer with a Christian club, which seemed to pique his interest.

It started with small talk and then he said he had been going to a local Christian church. He said, "I've never felt so comfortable in a church before."

I told him, "I was raised as a Catholic and didn't know how good a church could feel until I got into one that was truly spirit-filled. I realized what had been missing in my life was a personal relationship with Jesus. I found there was a difference between Christians who have a personal relationship with Jesus and those who only know *about* Him. I call them secular Christians."

Then the Holy Spirit went to work again. I could tell the guy was at his final stage of preparation for salvation (for the Lord prepares our hearts to receive him, as it says in Proverbs 16:1). He was open and eager to continue. I felt he could sense I knew something he didn't. I asked him, "Have you ever surrendered your life to Jesus, and asked Him to come into your heart through prayer?"

He replied, "No I haven't, I don't know anything about that."

So, I explained the basics of the Gospel of Jesus Christ to him and then told him, "There's a prayer, called the sinner's prayer, it's simply a confession of your faith in Jesus, acknowledging His sacrifice for all our sins, and your belief He rose from the dead. You can ask Him to come into your heart to guide you into righteousness and salvation, through your faith in Him."

Now, mind you, we were standing in the middle of a large group of tatted leathered-up bikers. This was not the type of environment conducive to one giving up any part of one's pride or ego. It takes what I believe to be a miracle for this to happen in private, let alone in public. However, I believe there is an almost irresistible urge to reach out for something your spirit says you can't live without.

After the Holy Spirit made His case, I told the guy, "The Bible says, if we confess with our mouth Jesus is Lord and believe in our heart He died for our sins and was raised from the dead on the third day, we will be saved according to Romans 10:9." I asked him, "Would you like to pray with me asking Jesus into your heart so you can collect the real prize?" He enthusiastically said, "Yes!"

Glory! Glory! Praise the Lord and how He works in such mysterious and wondrous ways. The guy won way more than $157 with his raffle ticket, that's for sure! Mercy! All we must do is to stay focused on the main deal (salvation), ask God to use us, and seek first His Kingdom and His righteousness. By doing so He will truly bring us the desires of our hearts. After a while, we will realize the things that bring us the most joy aren't material or carnal, but spiritual blessings that will have an eternal impact!

Not long after the fundraiser, Bernard called to tell me Terri was coming home. He asked if we would assist them with a motorcycle escort from King City to San Luis Obispo. It was about a 160-mile round trip for the escort. Terri was being transported to King City from Reno. She was badly injured from the crash and had remained hospitalized in Reno until she was well enough to make the trip home.

We were honored to assist. We were scheduled to meet Teri's transport ambulance in King City. We arrived after dark and made the hook-up on time. There were approximately twelve of us involved in the escort. Terri was partially paralyzed and mostly incoherent at the time, but we were told later by the medics that when Terri heard the roar of our engines around the ambulance, she went from a sedentary state to one of excitement. She was unable to communicate but heard a sound near and dear to her heart.

Once we got Terri to the medical rehab clinic in San Luis Obispo, she was put into bed by the med staff, and we were able to then assemble around her bed. As we did, Terri's eyes were open, and she seemed aware. After a little small talk and happy comments about the ride, I felt compelled to be a little blunt. I told Bernard

I needed to ask him something personal. I don't remember what I said but it was about their standing with faith. This led me to ask if we could pray for his and Terri's salvation. Some of us were already Christian believers and involved in motorcycle ministry.

I asked if everyone would pray the sinner's prayer together, confessing our faith in Jesus as our Lord and Savior, and asking Him to enter our hearts. Bernard immediately agreed and all those present agreed. Terri became very excited and made a few sounds as her body started to react. She appeared to be emotionally excited and willing. Then, everyone held hands around Terri's bed and prayed the sinner's prayer out loud together. It was the perfect ending to a perfect and exciting day.

38

STARBUCKS MEETING

ONE MORNING I had prayed for our ministry and some of the little issues we had been working on. I also prayed for a divine appointment and specifically asked for it to be a decision for Jesus.

Chapo had called me earlier and we agreed to have an impromptu officers' meeting at Starbucks. I had been working with our people to get them to be more punctual and they had already shown some improvement, but still needed a little work. In their former lives, they had little or no discipline, accountability, or structure. That day they were again late.

While I was waiting for them to show up, I went into Starbucks and got in the long coffee line. A guy behind me tapped me on the shoulder and referred to my back patch. He told me he thought what I was doing was cool. He said he had recently started praying every morning, just to start his day off right. I gave him one of our tracts as we talked. He saw it was my last one and said I should maybe save it for someone else. I told him no because the tract had been made especially for him. He chuckled and received it graciously.

The shop was full of commuters and locals grabbing their morning coffee. We soon got separated by the crowd. As we waited for our coffee, I could see the guy was reading the tract I had given him. So, I just walked over and asked him if he had ever given his heart to Jesus by praying a prayer like the one on the back of the card. He said no, he had never seen a prayer like it before.

The Holy Spirit gave me a few verses of Scripture and right there in a crowded coffee shop provided a moment of calm, and I offered to pray with him to receive Jesus as his Redeemer. He said yes and took my hand in a firm handshake. We got our heads closer together for a little privacy as I asked him to repeat the prayer with me. In front of God and all those customers he quietly prayed the prayer, giving his heart to Jesus. Then he looked at me with tears in his eyes and said, "That was the real deal, wasn't it?" I told him if he meant what he just prayed, then we would be standing shoulder to shoulder at the gates of heaven one day.

I then asked him his name so I could pray for him later. He was happy to oblige and said, "Man, this is hardcore!" He was so happy and almost in shock. He said he had felt something come over him when we prayed. I ministered to him for a short while and then we got our coffees and went our separate ways. He looked numb and in shock over what had just happened.

I was pumped! I felt like I had just won a fight or a major confrontation! In the spiritual realm or sense, I guess I had. He said his name was Richard. The information I gave him had all the instructions for what to do next with his new faith and belief. A divine appointment? You tell me! I had just prayed for a decision for Jesus only an hour before. I had even forgotten about it until the guy tapped me on the shoulder. He came to me! What are the odds of that happening? Like I say, sometimes we plant, sometimes we water, and sometimes we harvest. I prayed later to thank God and I told Him I wasn't trying to test Him. I was just hungry to win more souls for the Kingdom.

When my guys showed up a few minutes later I thanked them for being a little late that day! If they would have been on time the opportunity might have been missed. We then had our meeting and all the issues that had previously annoyed us were quickly and easily resolved. To God be the Glory!

39
5150 Todd

A number of years back I met a 1%er named Todd at a local rally. He was friendly and personable, and we got along right from the start. He turned out to be a good friend and one of our greatest advocates. He was inquisitive about our organization at first and had some good questions to make sure we were solid and trustworthy.

We were already accepted by his club, but he was considering a move into our area with the intent of starting a new chapter. Before long he put out the word of his club's desire to follow through. The news went out to all the local MCs and a meeting was scheduled. When the time came, the various clubs were to meet up at a clandestine location to discuss the issue and meet all the players. But where was Todd? The meeting was to be at 8:00 PM. The clock kept ticking. 8:30 came and went, then 9:00, then 9:30. The clubs began murmuring and became restless. Then we got word Todd was in jail. He had been picked up on a warrant after a traffic stop and the meeting was scrapped. This was no doubt embarrassing to Todd, but he was stuck in the slammer until his club could bail him out.

Somehow, word got out about Todd's club planning to move into the area and law enforcement turned up the heat, eventually causing their plans to be placed on hold. But the Lord had His plan for Todd. We stayed in touch and each time we met I was able to minister to him. I could tell the Lord was working on his heart.

Todd had been the go-to guy when his club had business that needed tending. He used alcohol, drugs, and women to satisfy his cravings, and "taking care of business" to satisfy his lust for violence.

I remember meeting him one time at a large annual rally one county south of us. He was all ablaze in his colors and was checking everything out. Due to his club status and reputation he expected to be greeted and acknowledged at events. But some bikers, when intimidated by a rep from a large club, tend to avoid them and not make eye contact. That doesn't work for guys like Todd.

On that day there were buildings at the fairgrounds designated for use by the vendors selling their goods. I was inside the main building talking with the president of another club when Todd walked up and joined us. He had his right arm in a cast at the time. He had broken it a couple of weeks before in a fight with three guys. He had also been shot in the foot in a subsequent altercation a short time later. As we made small talk, I noticed Todd's eyes change. His breathing accelerated and his anger became more intense. It was his 5150 look, meaning "psycho." When that happens, things always get interesting.

As we were talking, Todd said "I'll be right back." He had been staring at three patched guys from a small local club, waiting for them to approach and acknowledge him. To avoid looking at him they turned their backs to us which, unbeknownst to them, was a big sign of disrespect. Whether right or wrong, it's just the way it is. If you can't play by the rules, you'll get thrown out of the sandbox!

They were only about twenty feet away as Todd approached and told them to take their cuts off. They hesitated for a few seconds and said, "Aw man!" Then they saw his eyes and command presence.

He said, "I'm not going to tell you again!" One of the guys was wearing a sergeant-at-arms tag, so Todd focused on him. He then said to one of the other two "Gimme a pen, and you better have one." As the guy handed him a pen, Todd said to the SAA, "Hold out your arm." As the guy complied, Todd wrote a phone number on the guy's forearm and said, "Give this number to your president and have him call it immediately." He then gave them a brief but stern lesson on protocol and respect and then walked away. It takes some serious intestinal fortitude to have a broken arm in a cast and challenge three bikers to submit or else!

When Todd got back to us, he was livid, and you could almost see the adrenaline pumping through his veins. We watched as the three bikers walked out of the exhibit hall with their cuts folded over their arms and their tails tucked between their legs. Message received!

But there was another side to Todd. Not too long afterward he called me from another county, and we talked some more about the Lord. Then, to my surprise, he asked me if I would do a memorial service for a biker brother. I felt I needed to tell him I wasn't an ordained pastor to which he replied, "Well, I consider you *my* pastor!" And that was that. I agreed.

When the day came, we rode to a city north of us and got booked into a local motel. Soon afterward Todd and the son of the deceased stopped by our room. I could see Todd was getting more and more drawn into faith. So, not wanting to miss the moment, I related the message of salvation from the Book of Romans and asked if they wanted to give their hearts to Jesus. They both enthusiastically said yes. We gathered all our guys together with them and prayed the sinner's prayer. It was an uplifting moment. Then everyone took off for the service.

Every seat in the chapel was filled, not to mention those standing in the back! 1%ers were everywhere and everyone was anxious to get started. The Holy Spirit must have spoken the words they needed to hear because at the end I told them if they believed their loved one was in Heaven, there was only one way to be sure they would be reunited again, and that was to get right with God. Then I shared the sinner's prayer. Afterward, about fifteen club members and guests raised there hands acknowledging they had just accepted Jesus as their Lord and Savior. I'm telling you when God says "Go," you better go!

When I was done with my part, I opened the floor to anyone wanting to speak on behalf of their departed brother. Several people came forward and solemnly told their stories. Then this nervous guy comes forward and says his peace, ending with "We did a lot of [expletive] together," but I quickly interrupted and said over the microphone, "You can't say [expletive] in church," and everyone cracked up laughing. It was the perfect ending to a solemn occasion.

Before long I got another call from Todd asking me if I would marry him and his girlfriend. I checked with my church and the elders voted to authorize me to do weddings and signed a declaration to that effect.

I called the bride-to-be and discussed her faith. When we were done, she too accepted Jesus as her Lord and Savior. We got it done in a local clubhouse and all went well. The marriage produced a boy child but then ended within about four years. We had all done our best, but in the end "IIWII" (it is what it is).

Then one day I get another call from Todd. He was in trouble, not with the law but with his club. He had been outed and was summoned to meet up with his chapter brothers, but he didn't go. He decided instead to get out of town to get his head right. He said I was the only one he could trust. Hours later he was on my doorstep. Todd stayed with us for about three days. When he left for parts unknown, I told him to call and check in so we would know he was safe.

Before long I get another call from him, just checking in. As he updated me, he said, "Oh, by the way, I got shot." He went on to explain he was out and about one day and heard someone call his name. It was a former club brother. The guy approached him even as Todd told him to stay away and bounce. The guy wanted to hug him, but Todd again said "No, bounce!" He wasn't going to fall for an ambush. As the guy turned to leave Todd also turned away and then he heard shots ring out as he took a bullet through his upper leg. As close as they were, the guy had missed, but one of the bullets had ricocheted off the pavement, hitting him in the leg. The shooter then ran away and disappeared. Afterward, Todd laughed about it and thought it was funny. That's Todd! The shot had gone through and through and Todd recovered nicely.

After he got re-settled again, he called and told me he was relieved to be out of the club and how he had found a church he loved. He said he had also taken to the streets to bring people into the church so he could be a part of loving people who needed it the most. He has even bought clothing and shoes for the needy in his travels. He also found a good job that provides him with enough money to help support his son who he loves dearly. He has come a long way, that's for sure. We talk often and I've never seen him happier.

40

Sweet Louise

Louise Kuntz was one of my mom's best friends. I was visiting Mom one day and remember her telling me Louise's health was in decline. She had been admitted to Twin Cities Hospital several blocks away from Mom's apartment. I was really tired that day. I couldn't wait to get home and take my boots off. As I left Mom's place, the hospital was to the left and the freeway was to my right. I tried to turn right but felt like I just couldn't do it. It was like God had His hands on my handlebars. I relented and turned left toward the hospital. As I looked for Louise's room, I couldn't get it out of my head how strong the resistance to me making a right turn had been. I knew I was being directed to see her.

When I found her room, she lit up with a big smile as I entered and greeted her. She told me she wasn't doing too well. Once again, I felt a sense of urgency I had come to recognize. I started sharing with Louise and asked her if she wanted to invite Jesus into her heart as Lord and Savior. She said yes and took my hand as we prayed the sinner's prayer. Afterward, she seemed at peace. She then squeezed my hand and smiled saying, "I'm not afraid." I can't express how pleased I was to have submitted to the spiritual pull that caused me to turn left.

Louise passed away a short time later and Mom asked me to take her to the memorial service. It was held nearby in a little mortuary chapel named Chapel of the Roses. When we got there, only about a dozen or so friends and family members were present. Louise's daughter spoke about her mother and then asked if anyone had anything they wanted to say.

I waited for someone to raise their hand, but no one did so I raised mine. I was invited to come forward to the lectern to speak. Before I left home, I had prayed for an opportunity to tell someone about Jesus, and perhaps another divine appointment. I asked that if I had a chance to speak, the Lord would give me the words to touch someone's heart.

When I went forward it happened, the words just flowed. I took about ten minutes to deliver the Gospel message of salvation and to assure everyone how, although only God knows the heart, Louise had met the Lord's criteria for salvation by her confession of faith in Jesus as her Lord and Savior. I told them she and I had prayed together at the hospital. I also offered to pray the same prayer after the service with anyone present who wasn't positively sure where they are going after they die. I made sure to tell them how those who go to Heaven will one day reunite with loved ones there. When I sat down, I started praying silently for God to prepare a heart and bring the person to me. When the service was over, people started milling around, and several thanked me for speaking about Louise.

Once the room had completely emptied, my mom became restless and said, "Come on Lou, let's go."

But I whispered to her, "Be still."

Several more minutes passed, and she again said, "What are we waiting for? Everybody's gone, let's go."

Again I said, "Be still. Not yet." She sighed in submission.

Then a young man about thirty re-entered the chapel and came over to us and quietly asked me if I would pray with him privately. I told Mom I would be right back as I walked with the guy through the lobby to a private spot. When we stopped, I asked him if he wanted to give his heart to Jesus and he said yes. As we prayed together his eyes filled with tears. As always, it was a miraculous moment. He hugged me twice afterward and then asked me if it would be okay to hug me again. He was elated and could hardly contain his excitement. His name was Shon.

I gave him one of the same tracts I had given Louise in her birthday card the year before and had prayed with her at her bedside. I was pumped with adrenaline as usual and filled with joy at another miracle. It always blows me away. When someone says yes, they are exercising the free will God has given each of us. Truly amazing!

41

LISTEN TO THE SPIRIT BUT LOOK OUT FOR THE DEVIL!

I HAD JUST finished breakfast with our club officers and an hour later rode over to a friend's house to help him unload his Harley from a pickup. On the way back home, only a couple miles away, I was drawn to go to a Subway sandwich shop in town. I was arguing with myself, thinking I had just eaten earlier and wasn't hungry, so why on earth should I go into town for a sandwich? As I approached the intersection that would take me home, I was strongly motivated to go straight, not to turn left towards home, but to go to the stupid sandwich shop! I even argued with myself, thinking "This is ridiculous!"

As I went straight to cross through the intersection, a car ran the red light and blasted across in front of the Ford Bronco in front of me. We both hit our brakes, but the Bronco had anti-lock brakes and slowed quicker than I could because I was locked up and sliding with the momentum of 850 pounds of Milwaukee iron (the weight of my Electra Glide Harley). I steered to the left of the Bronco and passed him while in the skid. But I was still going straight and was in control. I smiled and waved as I went past the Bronco and the driver seemed to get a kick out of it. His eyes were bugged out and he was shaking his head about the other driver who almost wiped us both out. Whew, close call! Somebody didn't want me to make my destination but *Somebody* else did. I frequently pray for "one a day" to share my faith with and God is ever faithful in providing them. At the time though, I still didn't realize what was going on.

When I got to the Subway shop, I ordered one to go, thinking I would put it in the refrigerator and eat it later. On the way back to my bike I heard a voice from behind me. It was a guy named Murray I used to work with. He was an acquaintance, not particularly a close friend. He was "on the clock" at work but taking an early lunch break. It was about 11:00 AM.

As our conversation began, he told me about a recent motorcycle accident he had been in. It was his second. He said God must have a plan for him or something, but he didn't know what it was. He pulled out a St. Christopher medal and said he thought maybe it helped him, but he didn't know for sure. He opened the door for a spiritual conversation, and I walked through it with him. He told me he was raised Catholic and had at one time read the New Testament about six times.

This seemed impressive, but as he continued, I could see the words he read had entered his mind but not his spirit. He rejected the Bible now and said he believes men had altered it for political gain over the years and it was no longer trustworthy. He said he had been studying many different religions, among them Buddhism, Hinduism, and Islam. He said he felt the closest to Buddhism at the time.

I wondered why a person would believe one religion to be unreliable due to man's tampering with Scriptures and another religion would be considered reliable and untouched by corrupt man. The Holy Spirit came alive in me, and I realized Murray was my *one for the day*. I was led to discuss the Dead Sea Scrolls and a story about a friend who had compared those earliest examples of the Scriptures with one of today's translations and found the message of salvation to be virtually unchanged.

As the conversation continued, words flowed out of me so smoothly. They were non-confrontational words coupled with Scriptural verses. I kept feeding him the Word of God, knowing the words were so powerful they could penetrate the armor of a hardened heart. I knew only God could do what I could not. I'd seen this so many times before. Many times, Murray had no comeback. When he did, the Holy Spirit countered it. I had little to do with the whole thing other than being available and willing.

We must have talked for over half an hour. Before we parted ways, he told me he prays to God often and when he does, sometimes he cries. I told him it was God working on his heart, preparing him for the next step in his spiritual journey. I told him God was softening his heart for acceptance of the truth. I then retrieved one of our tracts from my vest pocket and asked him if he would accept it. He politely and willingly did so.

As we said goodbye he said, "I'm still asking God to tell me what He wants me to do."

To this, I replied, "He just did." Murray just looked at me speechless. He didn't know what to say. That's when I told him how I pray for one a day to share my faith with. I went on to relate about just having eaten breakfast, the near-miss accident, and not having a clue what I was doing at the sandwich shop when I wasn't even hungry. I told him God faithfully answers my prayers to serve Him by supplying the person he wants me to share His truth with. All I've got to do is show up and it is always permissive, friendly, and non-confrontational. He agreed how he enjoyed the conversation and how it was indeed non-confrontational. He thanked me sincerely and I sensed the conversation had a profound impact on him.

A serious planting was done that day and I got on my knees when I returned home and thanked the Lord for faithfully answering my prayers, and for the blessing of being used as His servant. I asked that the enemy be bound so the seed planted in Murray would not be blown away but would take root deeply as in fertile soil. I can't recall the exact specifics of what was said that day, but it was no doubt a divine encounter and a very powerful one. I had an adrenaline rush throughout the conversation and felt as if I were in a combat situation against the forces of evil—not Murray, but the enemy. I trembled inside at the excitement, but my countenance was calm and smooth. Sometimes we will experience a feeling like this in a spiritual encounter. It was very powerful, and I knew something special had just happened.

Murray was sewn with the seed of the Holy Spirit and is ready for the next believer to enter his path, to water, nurture, or maybe harvest. We never know where we are in this chain of events until the door opens. It was a special experience. We can't see into the soul because only God knows people's hearts, for it is He who prepares them!

We must stay alert and obedient, otherwise we could miss an opportunity to win a soul for the Kingdom of Heaven. I'm telling you, God is good! And we're just the messengers!

42
Hollister Runs and Shootouts at the Gas Pump

OVER THE YEARS the annual rallies at Hollister, California have always been a highlight. We had attended them annually from the beginning of the Last Disciples. Historically, the 1947 Hollister "Gypsy Tour Rally" was attended by over 4,000 bikers. It was held over the Fourth of July weekend and turned into what the press called a riot. It was where the "1% outlaw" biker identity was first coined. It meant that 99% of bikers are good law-abiding folks, but 1% are outlaws and misfits. Hollister is a small town south of San Jose. The biker history there goes back to the 1930s when they hosted uphill motorcycle races. Reams have been written on the history of the races and rallies near the quaint little town. If the reader is interested, much can be found on the internet about the topic.

For us, in the twenty-first century, Hollister is a fun, historical locale for independents and clubbers to come together to buy, sell, trade, socialize, eat, drink, and just soak in the history and excitement always to be found there. We never had a bad experience at this rally. But as times have changed so have the politics between some of the larger MCs. Conflicts can occur and sometimes do (no matter where you go). This has eventually led to some shootings over the years.

Whenever we roll into town, there is a gas station we always stop at to refuel and get snacks and drinks as we wait for our other members to roll in from their respective areas. Well, wherever there are bikers, alcohol, drugs, and politics, the chance of conflicts can increase. Now and then fate creates a perfect storm and enemies arrive at the same place at the same time and something is likely to go sideways.

On two of our runs to Hollister, two MCs rolled into this same gas station at the same time and words were exchanged. One thing led to another and then the bullets began to fly. One year it happened the day before we got there, and one year right after we had left. We were in the habit of always stopping at the same station on our way in, as well as on our way out of town. During both incidents, bikers were killed, and the wounded ones had to be medevacked out. I'm starting to lose count of the times *Someone* must have been watching over us.

While on the topic of Hollister, a special story comes to mind. One year, after leaving the rally, we stopped as usual to top off our tanks. Our guys had all hit it back home already and I was with our vice president, Pat Kelley. Pat has always been a prayer warrior and is always alert. Not much gets past him. He is the quiet type and frequently, if he sees I'm engaged in a conversation with someone, he will hang back and pray for the Lord's will to be done.

On this day, while gassing up, I noticed an elderly lady trying to get her credit card to work at the pump. She looked a little frazzled. I walked over, all leathered up, and asked her if I could help. She didn't seem bothered by my looks, most likely because the town was filled with thousands of bikers. I think the residents get used to seeing us each year. She seemed a little unsteady and sat down on the edge of her seat. I asked if she was alright and she said, "Not really." She went on to tell me she was recently diagnosed with terminal cancer.

I got her gas started and then took a knee next to her. I tried to comfort her and just knew in my heart I needed to ask about her faith. I told her I didn't want to invade her privacy but needed to ask her if she knew Jesus. "Not as well as I should," she answered. I told her how our purpose in life was to help people find their way to Jesus. It only took about five minutes to tell her the message I was given to share. She relaxed as calmness seemed to overtake her.

I then asked if she would like to ask Jesus into her heart to be assured of her destiny, whether the Lord heals her or not. I also assured her we will be able to reunite with our loved ones someday in Heaven, but we must first be sure we are right with God. She got excited and said yes. As I knelt beside her, she took my hand and repeated the sinner's prayer as she was led to a place of peace. I returned her credit card and finished refueling her car. She said she had a daughter in town who was helping her to get through her days. I then suggested she share the little tract with her daughter, and she excitedly said she would. I hugged her and told her I would be praying for her. As she drove away, she honked her horn with her hand out the window waving at us. It was so awesome.

God always provides. We need to stay healthy to be good and faithful servants. But not long after getting back from Hollister, I came down with the flu. I've never been so sick. I threw up for several days. I couldn't eat and was becoming dehydrated. I was lying across the bed late one morning, praying to the Lord for help. I told Him I felt like I was going to die. I remember telling Him if I could eat at all, the only thing I wanted was chicken broth and Jell-O.

About an hour or so later, there was a knock at my door. An elderly couple in their late seventies stood there. It was Gladys and Jim, friends and former neighbors of my mother. Gladys said she heard I was sick and couldn't get me off her mind. She had a basket in her hand and inside was, you guessed it, chicken broth and Jell-O!

I thanked them and had to choke back my emotions. I was so overwhelmed by God's mercy and grace.

Several weeks later I dropped by to return their containers. My mother had previously given them a book about faith and accepting Jesus as our personal Lord and Savior. We talked for a little while and the Holy Spirit took over as He so often does (when I don't get in His way). I began ministering to them.

Then, it was as if Satan was trying to distract us because as we were getting to the critical part of the message I was sharing, the front door of their apartment suddenly blew wide open. They looked a little startled since it wasn't even a windy day. It was still and sunny. I smiled and said, "Don't be bothered by that, it happens all the time, it's just Satan showing himself out." The three of us then joined hands and prayed the sinner's prayer together. It was a special and tearful moment. What a joy it was!

Gladys and Jim have grown in their faith, joined a local church, and are involved in community service. I am so happy for them!

43

THE GREENS – CRAZY DAN

AS WE TAKE to the highways and byways we never know where the roads will lead us. We network continually, always trying to expand into the world. As we do our meet-and-greet thing at rallies open to the public, we will usually meet members from other clubs. And *sometimes* the dominants will share their turf and tolerate others. It depends on the times, location, and politics.

As we work with crowds, we sometimes get invites from a dominant to attend a memorial service for a fallen brother, or maybe a fundraiser they're hosting. We always go where we are made welcome. We assume nothing but instead walk by faith, trusting the Lord will watch our six. At times we must walk a very fine line so as not to step on the toes of the ones who originally blessed us into the outlaw biker world.

On one occasion we were invited to a memorial service at a Sacramento veterans hall for a member of the Greens who had recently lost his life. We were given a warm greeting and welcomed as we worked our way through the mass of Green 1%ers after the service. There I met a member named Crazy Dan and we remain in touch to this day. Getting to know his club brothers eventually led us to a sit-down with their SoCal brothers, which in turn eventually opened a few more doors for us.

Speaking of Crazy Dan, I got a call from him one day that set me back on my heels a little. He told me he wanted me to know he was okay. I was a bit confused and asked him what had happened. He said, "Didn't you hear? I got shot on the I-5 going down south with my bro."

"Are you kidding me?" I asked. Then Dan went on to relate the following story:

> "Yeah, me and my bro were riding south on the I-5, rolling about ninety like we do, and there's this truck. Traffic was getting a little thick. I noticed it pull slowly next to me and I hear a "pop-pop" sound. The road was pretty noisy and with the helmet and wind and all, I couldn't hear what the pops were or where they were coming from. Then the truck is next to me again and I hear a louder "pop-pop-pop" and the sound of something hitting my bike. I was thinking the louder sounds must have been a .45 as the truck sped away."

Then Dan started working his way over to the right shoulder of the I-5 freeway. His clubmate was a little bit ahead of him at the time and had never even heard the shots. Once Dan pulled to a stop on the right shoulder, he put his kickstand down and removed his helmet. Meanwhile, his buddy had pulled over too and was rolling backward to see why Dan had stopped. Dan had begun looking his bike over. That was when he noticed bullet damage to his front forks and his rear cylinder barrel. As his partner walked over to Dan he said, "What's up?"

Dan told him what happened and then his club brother said, "Hey bro, you're hit!" Dan had never felt it, but one bullet had struck him in the side, and the projectile went all the way through his body and came to rest just under the skin on the opposite side. Dan said it was as visible as if a piece of cellophane was covering the bullet. He said you could even see the copper color of the bullet which had mushroomed to a larger size as it traversed through his body. It was a .45 caliber bullet.

The California Highway Patrol showed up soon and were shocked to find Crazy Dan was still on his feet. While waiting to be medevacked out, an Australian traveler stopped and approached them. He said he was a Christian and wanted to pray for Dan if it was okay. Dan said sure and the guy prayed. He then said God told him Dan would be okay. Then he left and drove off as the medevac arrived.

Dan went through three surgeries that year and completely recovered from his wound. One doctor said just about everything was hit in the bullet's path through him. He told Dan that when he first saw him, he didn't think his wound was survivable. But survive he did.

As Dan told me his story over the phone, I told him I felt compelled to ask him about his faith and if he was saved. To which he replied, "Oh heck yeah, I'm an ordained minister! I thought you knew." Go figure, I thought. What a crazy ministry we're in!

44
Greens in SoCal

Well, within a year of hooking up with the Greens up in Sacramento we got an invite to roll down to SoCal to meet some of their members down that way. We had a handful of guys living down there who knew a few of them. Always being ready for the next challenge, we gathered up and rolled down to Diamond Bar, 235 miles south of our chapter on the central coast. We hooked up with our Last Disciples SoCal crew when we arrived, then rode in a pack to a local bar where the Green event was being hosted.

There we met a few more of their officers. Our chapter president down that way was greeted warmly, but I was kind of brushed off. I didn't know what the problem was but left our president to visit with the Greens president and wandered into the bar with the rest of our guys. We stayed loose so it didn't appear we were grouping up out of insecurity or any ulterior motives. We were well received inside and greeted with handshakes and hugs. The effort was a formality and by the time we left, we had been made welcome to ride down in their area.

We must be careful not to get overconfident because Satan and his minions can always be lurking just around the next bend. You never know! Assume nothing and always follow protocol and the rules of respect. One wrong look or unthoughtful word could spell disaster. Our primary tool was prayer and waiting upon the Lord, trying to never get ahead of Him. As always, just like during our first sit-down, our churches were praying for us. The Lord is our strength and prayer is our go-to weapon of choice.

"Blessed be the Lord my Rock, Who prepares my hands for war, and my fingers for battle" (Psalm 144:1, NASB).

45
Last Disciples – East Side

"**Eastbound and Down**" as the song goes. Inquiries were coming in from all over the place. When the Lord opens doors, we always check out what or who's on the other side! We had been working our way across the US when one day I heard about a guy living in the Chicago area. His story was so intriguing I decided to make contact to see what he was all about. We must have talked for an hour-and-a-half. I learned he had been a 1%er, had an FBI number (meaning he has an FBI record), had run guns and drugs for very dangerous organizations, and at one point had to flee the Chicago area to protect his family since he was heavily involved in organized crime.

As always during first contact with a possible candidate, I ask them about their faith and belief system. He explained his story of conversion this way: "I was just minding my own business, and God showed up." He had been traveling around the world when this happened and decided to see where it took him. It led him to salvation and back to his wife after three years of separation. Having left his life of crime behind, he took a job as a janitor at her church and from there ended up in some deep street ministries, including prison ministry. His wife Beans was saved three years before him and started praying for him, which angered him to no end. My, my, how the Lord's plans come together! They have now been walking with the Lord for over forty years.

As we talked, I explained who we were and what we did. At some point in the conversation I said, "Oh, by the way, my road name is Raven." I could feel the depth of silence that came over him. After a moment he said one of the men he was ministering to, serving a life sentence for murder, had a dream. In the dream, there were hundreds of ravens all over the walls of the cell house and he woke up. The man asked him what he thought it meant. He said it led them to the Bible to search for ravens. They found them and concluded it would take a little more time for God to reveal what this might mean. As we talked, it was becoming evident to him I was somehow connected to the dream.

We had a very spiritual conversation as I presented the Last Disciples mission to him. As we continued, I asked if he would be interested in working together. Let me preface this by saying that after he was saved, having been a Satanist years ago, he went back to college and earned a Bachelor's degree, a Master's degree, and a Ph.D. in Philosophy. He had also become ordained.

He said he would pray about it. After months of fasting and prayer, he contacted me and said he was ready to merge into the vision. He had started many ministries, including Wiseguys and Deadman Killers who work with the most dangerous elements of society most churches are afraid of or ill-equipped to deal with, up to and including a couple of cannibalistic serial killers! He said he had leaders in place who could take over for him so he could concentrate on the Last Disciples. His road name is Ninja, formerly known as "The Freak" in his old life.

After his application process, he was thoroughly vetted according to our procedure. He also completed our Discipleship Program, which is required of all candidates. It is our way of knowing we are all on the same page. When he was finally patched, he went to work contacting the dominant in his area near Chicago and started having sit-downs, not just one, but many. The politics and protocols were very complex in his area, but Ninja knew the ropes well. He also had skills in administration protocol to help us get more organized. Under his guidance and leadership, the Last Disciples MC in the eastern half of the USA is growing at a rapid pace. Ninja and I concluded over the years that God is not done with us, and He is in total control. We are true spiritual brothers and great friends.

Ninja is a man who has been on both ends of a gun and knows how to stay calm and "unoffendable" during times of turmoil. The brothers he has brought into the Last Disciples are soul-winning men who are committed, with no compromise on the Gospel of Jesus Christ or our mission.

Our last national run was held in South Fork, Colorado. We had members coming from all over the country. Ninja rode solo as he often does around the United States. On this trip he rode through frequent rain, a mud and rock side in the mountains, eight hailstorms, a hurricane, sleet, and snow, all the way from Illinois to Florida and then west to Colorado. He even led a biker to the Lord while seeking shelter beneath an overpass.

Another member named "Tick Tock" rode in from Florida. "Tommy Gun" left New York after finishing work and rode straight through. Skeeter, our national secretary, rode in from Alabama. And Rocky rolled in from Oregon.

Speaking of Rocky, he had earned his name on a previous run when we came upon a big rockslide and he center-punched one he couldn't dodge. Danny Blade and I were behind the pack and saw the whole thing. He went airborne like a stunt rider but landed on two wheels, perfectly balanced, and wobbled to a stop where he put his kickstand down. The front mag wheel was smashed, his front forks were bent back to the motor and his frame was bent. His beautiful Harley Road King was totaled and un-rideable. But guess what? Danny Blade and I had a trailer behind my truck loaded with mine and Danny's bikes since we were running "chase vehicle" for the pack.

Our whole national crew, from the North, South, East, and West gathered in a big circle in a rest area just off the road and prayed, thanking the Lord for His traveling mercies. Next, we pulled Danny's bike off the trailer and loaded Rocky's bike aboard. While that was going on, I went secretly from man to man, quietly soliciting their vote on promoting Rocky to a full patch member. He had put in the time, and this was a perfect opportunity to lift his spirits. He got a unanimous vote, and we gathered around him and prayed him in on the spot. Everyone then started laughing and cheering. Danny got on his bike, Rocky jumped into the truck with me, and down the road we went with outlaw country music blaring on the XM radio station. It was great!

When we found a Harley dealership, we left Rocky's totaled bike with them and rented him another Road King to get him back on the road. Where there's a Last Disciple there's always a way!

We rented a huge log cabin in the Colorado mountains and had members and bikes everywhere! The two-story cabin was packed with brothers in hammocks, sleeping bags, and bunk beds. Everyone worked together as one big team buying and cooking food, running errands, and taking care of details.

In the mornings, Ninja would lead prayer and Bible studies, and in the evenings we would have our meetings to discuss our goals and long-term plans as well as regular club business.

On our first evening there I addressed the membership and spoke from the heart. I was getting older and had been lining people up in recent years to step into positions of authority, and to follow the vision we had laid out from the beginning. With the eastern half of the country developing nicely, we were now established coast to coast. I thought it was the perfect time to hand off the baton to another candidate for international president. I felt Ninja was the best qualified for the position and a motion was made to open the floor for other nominations. There were none and Ninja was voted in for the position.

I next asked that I be approved for the position of "National Nomad" and to remain as a voting advisor on the national board. My new position was approved unanimously. It was perfect for me. In this position, I could continue to keep our vision on track and troubleshoot any problems that might pop up while the everyday operations of the club went to Ninja.

The eastern USA was finally coming together, and we had all our national board positions filled by the time our gathering was over. This was something that took a huge load off my shoulders, and I was happy to still be in a leadership role. I needed the break after putting so much of myself into the demanding mission over the years.

46

Valley of the Shadow of Death

My last trip through the Valley of the Shadow of Death lasted three years! I had been attacked by an undiagnosed illness. My gym workouts had been six days a week. But then they slowly went down from there until there were none. I went through two separate teams of doctors and specialists. I finally ended up in the hospital. My blood was tested at the lab repeatedly. It was finally sent to the University of California Davis, and they found nothing. They said I had "Valley Fever" at one time but didn't have it then. In the end, after years of exams and a decline in my health, the doctors raised their hands, shrugged, and said, "We don't know."

I doubled down on praying. At one point I was pretty much housebound. I had zero energy and ached all over. I read the Book of Job again. Doing so always makes me realize how much better off we are than we may think at the time.

As I lay around every day I would read the Scriptures, pray, and watch the world news on television. I remained active throughout the whole ordeal, often working from bed. With my laptop, cellphone, and Ninja's leadership, we kept everything running. And Danny Blade, our faithful sergeant, never let me down. We had built up a bulletproof team of brothers who were committed and had each other's backs. I wanted to be sure if the Lord took me Home our ministry wouldn't skip a beat. I realized I had everything I needed and a great and loving wife in Reann who kept me fed and always encouraged me. I decided I was blessed and content with what I had. I needed nothing more.

Then, just as mysteriously as my health had begun its long decline, I started getting better, one day at a time. I was back in the game!

During the last two years of the illness, I also had a couple more melanoma surgeries, a complete shoulder replacement, a complete knee replacement, a neck procedure, another back surgery, plus hand surgery. I had also been attacked by two pit bulls at the front door of the post office, with injury to my right calf and right hand, and my little rat terrier Jax was almost killed.

It doesn't matter what the circumstances are, there is always hope and always a way. We must learn to find contentment in all circumstances, just like the Apostle Paul did. Stay focused and stay tuned. Tomorrow is a new day. Our prayers and resistance to adversity and evil will put us on higher ground. Stay in the fight and never quit. I may be getting old, but I am feeling great again and am far from finished, God willing!

47

Hard to the Core

To demonstrate the resilience and determination of some of the Last Disciples, I would like to mention the challenges faced by a couple of our members. I have already written about Robert "Chapo" Garcia. But I want you to know just how tough some of these guys can be. They are an inspiration to us all.

Chapo was one of our cofounders and lived one town north of me, in Paso Robles. He never missed an event. We rode all over the western states together and he was an awesome traveling partner. He always cared more about others than himself. As I mentioned earlier, he had become ordained over the years after having served six years in prison.

Chapo was a diabetic and had some serious extra wear and tear on his internal organs after years of drug and alcohol abuse. He was about six feet tall and stocky. As the years rolled by, he began having problems healing up after little cuts and minor injuries. He had to frequently check his blood sugar levels and his circulation was also taking a hit.

When I first met Chapo, he already had one of his toes amputated. In time, several of his fingers started turning black and he needed more amputations. The insidious disease was starting to eat him alive. I remember taking him to an LA hospital for impending finger surgeries. He was to be admitted for a few days while they ran tests on him. I returned home in the meantime and two days later

I got a call from Him. He was pretty upset. He said they had taken him into surgery to remove two fingers, but when he woke up his whole left hand was gone. Once they got into the operation, they said his hand was too infected and couldn't be saved.

I drove back to LA to pick him up and bring him home. Within a few months his toes started turning black. But Chapo had accepted his fate by then and he remained cheerful and upbeat. He never complained and never shed a tear. His pain was intense but when I would drop by to check on him, he would always greet me cheerfully and ask, "How you doin', Brother?" with a big smile. No matter what, he remained positive throughout his ordeal. He continually kept praising God. Chapo didn't know the word *quit*. It simply wasn't in his vocabulary. He would just laugh and tell of his plans to modify his motorcycle so he could keep riding and witnessing to the lost.

Chapo's kidneys started to fail at one point, so he was placed on dialysis. Both his feet had also started turning black. I loaded him up in my truck and we took off to LA again. His wife was still working and had to remain behind. About halfway there I pulled into a gas station rest stop so we could use the restroom. Chapo had an IV bag we hung from a sun visor in my truck. He was also confined to a wheelchair at the time due to his foot deterioration and pain.

I got his wheelchair set up and got him out of the truck, pushing him into the oversized men's room. People were coming in and out. I got him up to a urinal and he stood up to relieve himself. Then, suddenly he started wobbling and said, "Oh no, I'm dizzy." He then fell back into his wheelchair which tipped over backward and down he went onto the floor. I got down on my knees to help get him back up, as the other customers stared down at us. No one offered to help. It felt as if they thought we were defiled or something! I got him back up and into his chair, but no one spoke a single word to us.

When I got him back into the truck, I put his wheelchair in the back and hopped behind the wheel. We fastened our seatbelts and as I looked at Chapo we both busted up laughing! I said, "Can you believe it Bro, two tough bikers, not afraid of anything, groveling around on the floor of a public restroom, and everyone avoiding us like we've got the plague!" It was hysterical. I dropped the truck into gear and we hit the I-5 onramp southbound.

Again, I left Chapo down south and returned home. His legs were both amputated just below the knees and not long afterward a finger on his right hand turned black as sin and broke off in bed. Then, before long, they amputated his right arm just below the elbow.

There was my brother Chapo - no legs, no left hand, and half of his right arm gone. We continued visiting him and again he never whined or pitied himself. He remained cheerful. When you would visit, he always asked how *you* were doing and wanted to catch up. One day a group of Last Disciples gathered around his bed at home, and he told me to bring him his jewelry box from off the dresser. He had me open it and dig out his biker rings. He then picked out each ring and had me hand it to a brother member. As I did so he laughed and said, "You guys might as well have 'em, they're not doing me any good now!"

He was one tough brother! He had told me he had no pride left in him since he couldn't even go to the bathroom by himself. He couldn't bathe, brush his teeth, or even eat without help. But despite all that, he talked about getting prosthetics so he could keep going. He even talked about getting a Harley trike so he could still ride with us.

But before long Chapo was admitted to the extensive care unit at Twin Cities Hospital in Templeton. His loving wife Kathrine and ladies from their church would gather around his bedside and softly sing beautiful church hymns. The nurses told us they could feel a spiritual presence in the room, as if angels were watching over Chapo.

His wife Katherine stayed with him day and night, even sleeping on a couch in the lobby. One night at about 11:00 PM I got a call from her telling me that Chapo had just gone home to be with the Lord. God bless him, his fight was over.

The next example of a tough and tenacious Last Disciple is Joe "Magic" Perez. I first met Magic at a Reno biker rally. Our New Mexico crew had invited him to ride with them and hang around with us at the event. They had all rolled in together from Albuquerque. When we met, he looked like a guy who knew his way around the culture. He was dressed in all black and white clothing and wore a black and white bandana headband, folded wide, Chicano style.

We sat on a bench in the shade of a big refreshment tent. As we talked, our spirits connected. We were on the same track with the same mission and beliefs. We hit it off big time! It was the beginning of an enduring friendship.

Magic jumped through all the hoops required of new candidates and within a year he was voted in. He had been in a street gang and had a lot of street savvy. He also rode a big black Road King Harley with high "apehanger" handlebars. He had the look, the savvy, and the Lord! He was sold out for Jesus and was all in!

Like with Chapo, however, his previous life had taken its toll on him. His kidneys were shaky, and he was also diabetic. Since we are so spread out, we stayed in touch through the Marco Polo app, which makes it easier to talk from state to state and leave video messages of encouragement for one another.

Then the day came when both of Magic's kidneys had to be removed and he was placed on home dialysis. He had to plug a tube from a port in his abdomen into a machine for fifteen hours a day, every day! During that time, he would watch sermons on YouTube and listen to Christian music. He also planned on getting a new Harley to replace his old one. One day while on a dialysis break, he found the Harley he wanted and bought it. Here's another brother who doesn't know the word *quit*! He had also purchased a vintage T-Bird and during his therapy breaks, he had installed a lowered suspension, new wheels and tires, a custom steering wheel, and other parts. He also got it running and recharged the air conditioning system. Then he prepped the body for custom paint. He planned to use it for Low Rider functions as a witnessing tool. As I said, he's all in!

Then one day he stumbled over something in the garage and broke his ankle. So there he was, an energy-challenged diabetic, with no kidneys, on dialysis, and with a broken ankle. What more could go wrong, right? Well, as time passed his ankle was not healing properly and things were getting worse. It became so bad that the doctors had to amputate his left foot.

Without skipping a beat, Magic got fitted for a prosthetic limb, below the knee, and had it custom painted with our Last Disciples logo, in black and white colors. Like Chapo, he kept looking up. He had been putting out spiritual messages of encouragement on our members-only Marco Polo page. His messages were like mini-sermons, and they were always right on. There always seemed to be something you could relate to or needed to hear.

Also, during this time he bought a DJ setup for playing vinyl records and CDs on special occasions. He was planning on making it a little side business. This guy never stopped looking forward with enthusiasm.

Magic had been placed on a kidney transplant list and was still waiting for his number to come up. Then he contracted COVID-19 and it was bad, putting him back in the hospital and on oxygen. He was sick, real sick. Nonetheless, even in the state he was in, he kept putting out video devotionals from his bed almost daily. He refused to give in!

He recovered and finally made it back home. However, COVID-19 caused damage and hardening of the lower portion of his lungs, leaving him with a persistent cough. Yet still, he is home and planning to start a custom paint job on his latest Harley. I don't know how he does it! As Magic was going through his tribulation, we unanimously voted him in as our national chaplain, and he remains in that position as of this writing. He is still awaiting that new kidney.

48

REFLECTIONS

AS I THINK back over the last couple of decades, I realize what a ride it's been! All I wanted in the beginning was a Harley, to find a cool exciting ministry, and to ride with some like-minded brothers. Well, God granted my wishes. Then I wanted something tougher and more challenging. And again, God answered my prayers. I have learned that the tougher the ministry, the greater the enemy's resistance will be. We must be resilient and relentless.

As I've studied and ministered over the years, I have gained a little wisdom. For one thing, being a good Christian isn't for sissies! I found out how sometimes life can be good and I would be on an upswing, and sometimes things can take a nosedive and we don't understand why. The Lord has His reasons and there is a purpose for the highs and lows we go through. I now realize God is not always our personal sugar daddy. Sometimes He's a disciplinarian. Sometimes He's a drill sergeant. Sometimes He will ignore us for a while when we are being petulant. Life is not always all about us!

If we ask ourselves what a perfect Father would be like, the answer would be Jesus. Sometimes He will embrace us with love and compassion, and at other times He may say, "Gird up your loins like a man and toughen up" (Job 38:3 paraphrased). It takes grit, determination, and submission to be a faithful disciple.

I've also come to realize that if we don't learn our lessons well, we may just have to go back through them again. Suffice it to say,

God doesn't make mistakes. Sometimes He's merely waiting for us to get in sync with Him. He deserves unwavering worship and *respect*. And often He may just have a better plan. Of course, some things we will never understand this side of Heaven. He's God, we're not. So, what do we do? We press on, trust in the Lord "...and lean not on your own understanding" (Proverbs 3:5, NKJV).

We must remember Satan and his legions of demons are continually working to bring us down and pull us away from our faith. Resist him and hold every thought captive to the obedience of Christ (2 Cor 10:5, NASB). Jesus is our go-to refuge of strength, our Rock! We've got to dismiss all negative and ungodly thoughts. Obedience to God's laws, which are written on our hearts, brings inner peace. By loving and helping one another, we take the focus off ourselves and life becomes more meaningful. Lastly, avoid complacency and strive to learn more as you pray for wisdom and discernment. We will all be out of here in the blink of an eye. Our souls will be absent from our bodies and we will be in the presence of the Lord! If you haven't done so already, make a commitment in prayer today to stand strong with the Lord and never give up!

I am a Last Disciple, *and so are you!* Think about it. The world is getting crazier as we get closer to the end of days. More spiritual evil is being manifested daily. It's in our faces. We can't bury our heads in the sand! We may very well be the *Last Disciple* to share the message of salvation with someone before they are called to judgment! The Bible says we are to "go into all the world and make disciples of every nation." But you don't have to be a foreign missionary, the lost are all around us right where we are!

Enjoy your ride through life, remember to smell the coffee, and don't just keep the faith—share it! Until we meet again...

Acknowledgments

I **want to** thank and acknowledge some of my friends and family who have inspired me to write this book about my rather unique life and calling to ministry and using our spiritual gifts to glorify God. Most importantly, I want to thank my wonderful and loving wife, Reann, who has had to live with a guy whose days are filled with ministry duties, mental multitasking, and dealing with an aging body and all the associated aches and pains that come with it. Reann is a coeditor and put in the time to see this project through to completion.

I also want to thank Pastor Tom Farrell of the Atascadero Bible Church in Atascadero, California, who has been my pastor for over two decades. Thanks as well to Pastor Dave Rusko of the Paso Robles Bible Church in Paso Robles, California, who volunteered to mentor me when I first began my search for where and how the Lord wanted me to serve. Thanks also to Pastor Ron Smith, President of Global Sharing, who has been a faithful friend and supporter from the very beginning.

Hugely influential in my ministry life and direction was Pastor Robert "Chapo" Garcia. I first met Chapo at a church function in Santa Maria. I was standing by myself in the parking lot when he briskly approached me wearing all black leather, hair pulled back, a Fu Manchu mustache and soul patch, tattoos, and a leather-clad crew that looked like a death squad. I stood my ground and wondered what would happen next. When he got to the boundary of my personal space he smiled and offered his hand. That was the beginning of a mission I had no clue about. Thank you, Brother Chapo, and may you rest in peace, my beloved brother.

A special thanks to my good brother, "Ninja," who worked tirelessly with us on the editing. He is also the International President of the Last Disciples MC. I also want to thank Tim Couts, my computer specialist who patiently kept me up and running from beginning to end.

I can't write this section without acknowledging my brother Mike and my sister Connie, both believers and much-beloved blood kin. Connie led me to the Lord over twenty-five years ago by simply handing me a little Billy Graham tract, which I read (then prayed) before going to sleep that night. Thank you, Sis! And shortly thereafter Mike invited me to attend church with him at the Atascadero Bible Church. That was the beginning of my new life.

I want to thank my awesome Son, Ryan, for his unwavering love and support. He has proven to be the best of the best. We ride together and chow down often along the scenic and historical Highway 1 along the California coastline. Thank you my son for never causing me a moment's worry.

And last, but not least, I want to thank my mom, Anne, and my dad, Lou (senior). May you both rest in peace. They took me to church as a youth, loved me for who I was, and taught me right from wrong, even though early on I chose to be a rebel rather than a saint.